# 1 Piece of Advice™

# 1 Piece of Advice™

Exceptional women from around the globe
inspire you to unlock your potential.

Patricia J. Moser-Stern
&
Barbara K. Moser

**Library and Archives Canada Cataloguing in Publication**

Moser-Stern, Patricia J.,
1 piece of advice: exceptional women from around the globe inspire you
to unlock your potential / Patricia J. Moser-Stern & Barbara K. Moser.

ISBN 978-0-9810832-0-9

1. Women—Biography. 2. Successful people—Biography. 3. Leadership in women.
I. Moser, Barbara K., II. Title. III. Title: One piece of advice.

CT3235.M68 2009    920.72    C2008-907111-5

Design by Fortunato Design Inc.

Printed and bound in Canada by Friesens

**ENVIRONMENTAL BENEFITS STATEMENT**

**1 Piece of Advice** saved the following resources by
printing the pages of this book on chlorine free paper
made with 10% post-consumer waste.

| TREES | WATER | ENERGY | SOLID WASTE | GREENHOUSE GASES |
|---|---|---|---|---|
| 2 FULLY GROWN | 646 GALLONS | 1 MILLION BTUs | 107 POUNDS | 197 POUNDS |

Calculations based on research by Environmental Defense and the Paper Task Force.
Manufactured at Friesens Corporation

# Table of Contents

## Enriching the Soul

## Spotlight

## Reach for the Stars

# To Serve and Protect

# In the Pursuit of Knowledge

# Introduction

This book was created as a way to acknowledge and celebrate the accomplishments of women around the globe and to tap into the insight of these amazing women. It is also meant to encourage women from around the world to accept that they can achieve anything they want if they believe in the possibilities. This book provides *1 Piece of Advice*™ signposts, which are all pointing the way to your own success.

We began this journey because we were tired of hearing all the pundits reporting statistics and writing articles about the decline in women's prominence or inability to "break through" in a variety of fields. This is not to say that there are overwhelming numbers of women who have "made it" and therefore imply that barriers for women are illusionary. We have encountered both the tangible and intangible hurdles in our own corporate climbs.

By reaching out to trailblazing women across the world, we hope that what we're providing through this book is an antidote to the "glass ceiling" assertion. We intended to showcase that with persistence, courage and passion, women can and have achieved significance and success in many different areas. Believing that you "can't" will become a self-fulfilling prophesy.

What should amaze those reading this book is how many women have achieved prominence in a vast array of fields. When we started this project, we believed that we were quite knowledgeable about women who have "made it." However once we began researching what women have accomplished throughout the globe we were, quite honestly, astounded.

One evening while we were surveying our lists, we looked at each other and almost in stereo said, "Who knew?" and we recognized that this was part of the problem. Although women had accomplished much, they weren't being regularly touted in the media, nor did they seek out the spotlight—most were quite content to make a difference in the world without any fanfare.

So we began writing letters to these amazing women on a "wing and a prayer," while of course keeping our day jobs. In addition to our independent efforts, every Wednesday night we got together and became the ultimate production line—printing letters, stuffing and sealing envelopes. We sent the letters in batches over a 1 year period.

We didn't know any of these women personally—just by reputation. In our letters we explained the project and asked for *1 Piece of Advice*™ which they believed would inspire women to turn their dreams into realities. We explained that the *1 Piece of Advice*™ was meant to cause others to consider their possibilities from a different vantage point, and that it could be a word, a sentence or a paragraph.

When we went to the mail the first batch of letters, we took a deep breath, said a little prayer, and dropped them into the mailbox. The emotion it evoked was akin to that sense of joy and dread you experience when you take your child to their first day of school—knowing you need to do it, but also recognizing that you no longer have control over the outcome.

And then we waited. Imagine our joy at receiving responses just two weeks after we sent out the first letters! It was intense. We began getting replies both by regular mail and by email.

Follow up letters were sent to those we hadn't heard from after a couple of months—we hoped that perhaps as more and more women joined us on our journey, others would as well. Some did, some didn't. But quite honestly we were thrilled with the number of responses that we did receive.

Countless late nights and early mornings of work ensued in order to capture not only the wisdom of the words themselves but also to present them in the context of the contributors' lives. The simplicity and truth that speaks from the pages of experience of these women is profound. By understanding the challenges they faced and overcame, we too will learn. It is now up to all of us to honor their achievements by creating some of our own.

Our recommendation is to read the profiles of these renaissance women and their accompanying *1 Piece of Advice*™. Allow yourself to become inspired by the words and incorporate into your life, every day or every week, a Piece of Advice that resonates. Work your way through the book and see how it changes you and your possibilities. You can record your approach and triumphs in the *Reflections* section.

We believed that we could bring this book to life and against many odds we did. Every time we hit a "Road Closed" sign, we found a different route which inevitably brought us to a successful conclusion.

Never forget, the only time you fail is when you stop trying!

*Patricia J. Moser-Stern & Barbara K. Moser*

Joanne Thomas
Yaccato
*Canada*

Heather Reisman
*Canada*

Jayne-Anne
Gadhia
*England*

Val Ackerman
*USA*

Genevieve
Thiers
*USA*

Suzanne
Nora
Johnson
*USA*

Isabel Bassett
*Canada*

Sharon Allen
*USA*

Beth Brooke
*USA*

Colleen
Barrett
*USA*

Blossom
O'Meally Nelson
*Jamaica*

Adriane M.
Brown
*USA*

Helen
Gurley Brown
*USA*

Susan M.
Ivey
*USA*

# Corner Office

The term "corner office" was coined some years ago and is primarily considered a reference to the position of a senior executive within a corporation. The women in this segment have attained great success in business in a variety of fields. They arrived at their current destinations from many different directions.

Some have made their way through major corporations; others have chosen an entrepreneurial approach to the pinnacle. Each has an inspiring story and *1 Piece of Advice* that will be of value whether you are looking to make your way in the world of business or in another profession.

**Maha AlGhunaim**
*Kuwait*

**Kiran Mazumdar-Shaw**
*India*

# Val Ackerman

## President USA Basketball, USA

VAL ACKERMAN's path to becoming one of the most influential women in sports was not without some off-ramps, but she ended up right where she started—sports.

Val was one of the first women to receive an athletic scholarship to a US University. She was a four-year starter for the University of Virginia's basketball team, a three-year captain and a two time Academic All-American. Val earned her degree in political and social thought in 1981.

She followed her passion for law, after a one year stint as a professional basketball player in France. Graduating from the University of California School of Law in 1985, she spent the next two years as an associate for a Wall Street law firm.

Val's next job would change her life, career and the future of women's basketball. She joined the National Basketball Association in 1988, where she served as an attorney and senior executive for eight years. Once more, she was in an organization that was very male-dominated in the upper levels of management, but she loved the environment—working with a group of people who were very passionate about their work. The only challenge she did encounter was when she had her first child, as there was no one in this office environment who knew what it was like to juggle both work and family. However, as with everything she does, Val became adept at becoming a working parent.

There had been attempts by others to launch a professional women's basketball league in the past, but it wasn't until Val's stewardship as the Founding President of the Women's Basketball Association in 1996, that professional women's basketball became a reality. She shepherded the league to excellence and then in 2005, when it was well established, she moved to take on the Presidency of USA Basketball, becoming the first woman to hold this position. In this role, Val oversees the men's and women's national teams that represent the US in international competitions, including the Olympics.

Val is a strong proponent of ensuring that girls and women get equal opportunity to funds allocated to schools and universities for sports programs. She has seen the benefits of the law ensuring this equal opportunity with her two daughters.

She sees sports as teaching important life lessons such as teamwork and leadership. There is no question that these qualities are evident in Val's actions every day.

Courtesy of USA Basketball

*"Every day is a new start. It's never too late to change, correct, improve, apologize or expand your horizons. Live for now and without regrets."*
—Val Ackerman

# Maha AlGhunaim

## Chairperson and Managing Director Global Investment House, Kuwait

MAHA ALGHUNAIM has built an admirable reputation for herself, one that extends beyond the Arab business community. It all came about several years ago when she chose to start her own corporation. After working for 20 years in large financial concerns in Kuwait, Maha decided to establish an investment company that reflected her personality.

Her incentive stemmed from her keen understanding of the markets' needs, and acknowledging the vast opportunities and potential that lay untouched for the Arab financial markets. Reputable organizations took notice of Maha's savvy business accomplishments, with Forbes naming her one of the Top 50 Leading Arab Women as well as Maha being a regular on the Forbes 100 Most Powerful Women in the World list. The Young Arab Leaders organization has appointed her President of the Kuwait Chapter and she has been recognized as one of the top 100 Most Influential Arabs. She is a member of several Boards.

Maha founded Global Investment House with an underlying objective to meet the high expectations of regional and international clients and to enhance the investment services industry in the region. After continuous growth, Global is now listed on the Kuwait, London and Bahrain Stock Exchanges as well as on the Dubai Financial Market.

She obtained her Bachelor of Science in Mathematics from San Francisco University in 1982 and considered two career path options—to either continue her studies and become a university professor or enter the world of finance. She chose the latter. Maha accepts the fact that a "glass ceiling" exists, although she believes that you can get beyond first impressions. "When you start to speak professionally, in a language which your client needs to hear from you, your gender does not matter anymore. What really stays with them is what you achieve for them"*

Maha is a mother of four and knows the challenges in juggling work and family. She believes that family understanding and support from her husband are important factors that have aided in her success. Her philosophy on ensuring the young women of today become leaders of tomorrow was captured in a speech she gave in 2007: "Our daughters must be raised to be confident enough to take charge of their life—they can only do that if they have education in their right hand and ethics in their left hand."*

Courtesy of Global Investment House

*"My advice to women is to emphasize networking. Having good relations with influential individuals, and senior officials in organizations in different countries has enabled me to obtain crucial information, gain insight on new investment opportunities, and secure deals.*

*These relations have also helped me place our products and services in addition to launching myself and Global Investment House 'Global' in the financial world. A significant network of relations is a prelude to prominence; not having one will make you a soldier, but never a general."*

—Maha Al-Ghunaim

* From: *Glass Ceiling Does Exist in Kuwait*, Kuwait Times, June 6, 2007

# Sharon Allen

## Chairman, Deloitte LLP, USA

It's been quite a ride for SHARON ALLEN going from a small town in Idaho to chairing Deloitte's board by 2003. She is the highest-ranking woman in the firm's history and the first woman to serve as chairman of a leading professional services firm. In her role at Deloitte, she has responsibility for the governance of an organization with more than $10 billion in annual revenues.

Sharon grew up on a farm in Kimberly, Idaho (population 2600), the youngest of four girls. She did not play sports but participated in just about every other activity, including the debate club and drill team. While growing up, Sharon thought about being a nurse or a teacher.

Her studies took her to Moscow—Moscow, Idaho, that is. At the University of Idaho, she started out as an education major, but her roommate studied accounting. Out of curiosity, she took an accounting course and was hooked. Sharon discovered that accounting allowed her to combine her technical and analytical skills with her desire to work closely with people. So she switched her major to accounting and never looked back.

Early on, Sharon realized she needed to step outside of her comfort zone and take risks to be successful. In 1994, she was happy leading Deloitte's Boise office and becoming the first woman elected to serve on the organization's U.S. board. But for her career to take flight, she knew she had to spread her professional wings. An opportunity arose in Portland, Oregon, and two years later, another one in Los Angeles to lead a Deloitte region that was larger than her hometown! Sharon has found that when you step outside your comfort zone a funny thing happens—the new place begins to feel comfortable before you know it and that's when it's time to look for the next challenge.

She has benefited from strong mentors in her life, including her great-grandmother, who was one of the first female legislators in the State of Idaho. As Sharon benefited from her mentors, she is committed to giving back by mentoring others to help them with their careers.

Sharon has been honored for her contributions to business and community leadership, and has been a regular on the Forbes 100 Most Powerful Women in the World listing. She also believes strongly in volunteerism and as such has earned the Los Angeles Chamber of Commerce Distinguished Business Leader Award. She serves as a board member on the National Board of the YMCA and The Autry National Center. Sharon is also a member of the Women's Leadership Board at the John F. Kennedy School of Government at Harvard University.

Sharon's career trajectory offers a case study in persistence, hard work, common sense and humanity. She believes strongly in helping others to be successful, which is her way of honoring those who assisted her along the way.

Courtesy of Deloitte LLP

*"**Take responsibility for your own career**: Early in my career, I was passed over for a promotion. I went to my boss and shared with him a list of my accomplishments. He didn't know that I had done all of those things. The lesson—don't assume that the people you work for are aware of all the 'good work' that you are doing. Find a way to let them know without being a braggart.*

***Have a Mentor and be a Mentor**: Having a mentor— or, in my case, a number of mentors—was absolutely critical in shaping my career. A good mentor cares about you as a person, is interested in your success and provides a perspective you may not have considered. And don't forget that it goes both ways. Along with finding a mentor, be a mentor. Help others along the way, and you will feel more rewarded in your career.*

***Seek balance to do what's right**: How you act on your values determines your reputation and, ultimately, your success. But if you're totally dependent on your career for personal fulfillment, you may be tempted to cut corners if things go awry. Maintaining the proper balance in your life helps you to do what's right. By keeping your work in perspective and staying true to your personal values, you can maintain the strength of your convictions."*

—Sharon Allen

# Colleen Barrett

## President Emeritus, Southwest Airlines, USA

Given the pressures of escallating fuel costs, intense competition and rising customer expectations, it is almost inconceivable that the most profitable major airline in the United States is also the one which boasts the fewest number of passenger complaints. That carrier is Southwest Airlines, a billion dollar plus organization which serves over 100 million customers a year. In a time when many of the major airlines are floundering, what does Southwest have that the other carriers don't? The answer is quite simple—they had COLLEEN C. BARRETT guiding them for 30 years.

Until July 15, 2008 she was President and Corporate Secretary for Southwest Airlines Co., a high-frequency, low fare, point-to-point airline. Colleen's unique contribution has been the infusion of her acute personal sense of customer satisfaction into her role as head of the organization.

According to Colleen, her mother deserves the credit for developing her values and her sense of hospitality. Her mother imparted the importance of "Golden Rule" behavior—"Do unto others as you would have them do unto you." Even though her family was far from wealthy, her mother emphasized that it was important to have a giving heart for there were always people in greater need than you.

Colleen joined Southwest Airlines in 1978 as Secretary of the Corporation, after working for several years as Executive Assistant to Herb Kelleher (Southwest's Founder and Chairman Emeritus) at his law firm. Colleen has described Mr. Kelleher as a generous, inclusive man and a wonderful mentor. She credits him with providing her with many opportunities she came to fully appreciate later in life.

As Colleen progressed through the organization, serving as Vice President Administration from 1986 to 1990, Executive Vice President Customers from 1990 to 2001 and as President from 2001 to 2008, she became known as the "beating heart" of the company. Another description frequently applied to her is a "selfless leader" with a tremendous sense of altruism. When you combine this with her determination to get things done and her ability to directly and personally solve any problem thrown her way, then you have a phenomenal leader.

Yet it is her devotion to the welfare of her employees and their wellbeing for which she is most recognized. The results are that her genuine, unwavering loyalty and faith in her staff translates naturally into heightened levels of customer satisfaction and ultimately profits for the corporation.

Colleen is devoted to both her son and grandson. She is active in numerous civic and charitable organizations in Dallas, Texas and sits on several boards and commissions.

Colleen has remained true to herself and her core values: honesty, hard work and treating others with respect. It is probably safe to say that there are not too many other heads of highly profitable, major corporations who define "success" as their ability to "make a positive difference and to give back to someone."

*"Never take a job for the pay or title—take it only because you have a passion for the cause to which the company or organization is dedicated. Then it just doesn't feel like work and you will find that success is easily attained because you are completely committed to what you're doing."*
—Colleen C. Barrett

# Isabel Bassett

## Author, Broadcaster, Politician, Philanthropist, Canada

ISABEL BASSETT's contribution to women's leadership spans the roles of teacher, author, journalist, politician, broadcaster and philanthropist. She has and continues to use her influence to open doors for those without status or connections.

Isabel began her career as an English and French high school teacher, but soon switched to journalism as a newspaper reporter. During this time she also went back to university to obtain her Master's in English. Her thesis became a book called *The Parlour Rebellion*, that spoke of outstanding women of the later 19th and early 20th century.

While on her book tour, she was approached to audition for a TV show. This began her career in broadcasting. Over the years, Isabel focused her reporting on social issues, and produced challenging documentaries such as *No Fixed Address*, *Growing Up*, and an unflinching look at sexual harassment in the workplace in *Everybody's Problem*.

Isabel entered politics in Ontario, Canada in the mid 1990's and was appointed the Cabinet Minister responsible for Citizenship, Culture and Recreation. In 1999 she was appointed as Chair and CEO of TVOntario, the first woman to lead a broadcaster in Canada. During her 6 year tenure at TVOntario she continued to empower and create opportunities for women and encouraged diversity both in front of and behind the camera.

She was the first woman chair of Ryerson University's Board of Governors, where she spearheaded the establishment of an employment equity policy. When President of the Canadian Club, a highly-respected forum for leaders in politics, business, social development and the media, Isabel initiated a change in membership policies opening it up to women and visible minorities.

Her service to the community has included acting on the Board of Advisors for the Canadian Foundation for AIDS Research, Director of Toronto Women in Film and Television, National Co-Chair of The James

Robinson Johnston Chair in Black Canadian Studies at Dalhousie University. She has been honored by the YWCA as a Woman of Distinction.

Isabel currently writes, mentors and speaks about women's issues. She is also fund-raising for the York University Library, and the YWCA's innovative new housing project for low-income women.

*"If I can give only one piece of advice to young business women, I want to pass on what someone told me when I was starting out. I have never forgotten it, because it is advice that has served me so well through my years as Minister of Culture and as CEO of TVOntario, and I hope it will do the same for you.*

*It's very simple really. When you start something, settle on three objectives you want to achieve. Having thoughtfully established this course of action, do not allow yourself to be sidetracked by the many other worthwhile things you may wish to do, or be pressured by others to do. Work continually towards your goals. Even though you may face challenges along the way, your three objectives will be like beacons and guide you on your journey to success."*

—Isabel Bassett

# Beth Brooke

## Global Vice Chair, Ernst and Young, USA

BETH BROOKE has always loved sports, but one day during high school she was told by a doctor, that due to a degenerative hip disorder she would never walk again. Yet Beth never accepted the doctor's "inevitable" as acceptable. And she proved this doctor more than wrong, by excelling in athletics and being awarded a basketball scholarship to Purdue University, where she majored in industrial management and computer science. The attitude of challenging herself, never accepting a negative outcome and not taking the "easy way" has defined Beth's life and career.

So, it's no surprise that Beth made it all the way from Kokomo Indiana to Global Vice Chair of Public Policy, Sustainability, and Stakeholder Engagement, at Ernst and Young, one of the largest professional services firms in the world. She is one of the top female executives at the company and has been a fixture for three years on the Forbes magazine list of the 100 Most Powerful Women in the world.

Within Ernst & Young, Beth has been seen as an innovator and force for positive change. She spearheaded the creation of the Ernst & Young Corporate Responsibility Group, including its Fellows Program, which enables the firm's employees to spend three months working with aspiring local entrepreneurs in developing countries. She has also been a long time advocate of women's initiatives, diversity, inclusiveness and workplace flexibility.

Beth's policy expertise has enabled her to make strong contributions to the government sector as well. During the Clinton Administration, she worked in the U. S. Department of the Treasury, where she was responsible for all tax policy matters related to insurance and managed care. She played important roles in the healthcare and Superfund reform efforts.

A CPA and an FLMI, Beth has a B.S. degree from Purdue University. Throughout her career, Beth has been actively engaged in numerous civic and business organizations. She is a member of the inaugural class of the Henry

Crown Fellows of The Aspen Institute and a member of the Committee of 200. She serves on the Boards of TechnoServe, The White House Project and The Committee for Economic Development, The Atlantic Council of the United States, and the Partnership for Public Service. She also serves on the Harvard Kennedy School Women's Leadership Board, the Purdue Homeland Security Institute, the Advisory Council for the Open Compliance and Ethics Group, Advisory Board of the Women Leaders Program of the World Economic Forum, and the National Women's Leadership Hall of Fame Advisory Council. She is the recipient of numerous local awards, most recently the University of Michigan's 2006-07 Women in Leadership Award.

Courtesy of Ernst & Young

*"Every woman, at any point in her life, has a platform. It may be the job you have; it may be your role in the community or even in your family. It looks different at different times, at different stages and depends on many things. But we all have one.*

*The Rutgers women's basketball team used their platform as collegiate student athletes to speak out about an injustice which had a powerful impact on our nation and its values.*

*Successful women use their platform all through their life to affect and lead those around them to a better place, bringing about positive change. Think about what you do in your life and always be sure you are truly using the platform you have to make a difference…however big or small."*

—Beth A. Brooke

# Helen Gurley Brown

## Author, Editor-in-Chief, Cosmopolitan Magazine, USA

American author and editor HELEN GURLEY BROWN is an icon of the feminist movement of the sixties. She first achieved prominence for her 1962 book *Sex and the Single Girl* and in 1965 she became the editor-in-chief of the then faltering Cosmopolitan Magazine, which she transformed into a sexy, upbeat, top-selling magazine for young women in more than 27 different countries.

She was born in 1922, in Green Forest, Arkansas and lived in Little Rock Arkansas until her father, a school teacher, was killed in an elevator accident leaving her mother to raise Helen and her sister (who was partially paralyzed by polio).

Helen Gurley Brown never liked the looks of the life that seemed to have been programmed for her—"ordinary, hillbilly and poor," and in 1939 struck out and began attending the Texas State College for Women (1939–1941).

Her first job was at a radio station where she answered fan mail for six dollars a week, followed by working as an executive secretary at a talent agency. During this time (1942-45), secretaries were required to use the back stairs because the ornate lobby staircase was only for clients and/or male executives.

Helen Gurley Brown began her string of "firsts" back in 1948 when she became the first woman to hold a copywriter position at Foote, Cone & Belding, a Los Angeles advertising agency. She won two advertising copywriter's awards during her ten year tenure at the firm because of her ability to produce bright and eye-catching prose.

She skyrocketed to prominence in 1962 with her book *Sex and the Single Girl*, which came to symbolize the sexual revolution and Gurley Brown's own contention that women can have it all—love, sex and money—at a time when some magazines still insisted that "nice girls" only had two choices—"marry him or say no." Upon becoming Editor-in-Chief of Cosmopolitan Magazine, she made it the "must have" magazine of the single women, which it still is today. Although no longer Editor-in-Chief of the US Cosmopolitan, she still retains that role for the international editions of the magazine.

Helen Gurley Brown has been married to David Brown since 1959. She makes 86 look youthful. Still working and writing (she authored the book Sex and The Office in 2004), she continues to challenge, provoke, cajole and inspire every day.

Courtesy of Helen Gurley Brown

*"My piece of advice is to find some kind of work you can do real good, get satisfaction from and be so good at it that people will pay you to do it! Doesn't have to be 'fancy' work like writing or acting or singing; not even being great with numbers or persuasion. If this satisfying work gets you out of bed every day and on to its pursuit; if you get valued for it and paid for it, you can be a pretty happy person.*

*After I'd been a secretary since 16 and had 17 secretarial jobs, I got to be 33 and started writing advertising copy. I got the job because I wrote good letters to my boss, the head of the agency, so he let me switch to something more creative.*

*If you're good with food, I think you could go work in a restaurant as a hostess or maybe start a catering service from your home. I just find that getting up to go to a job where they need you is a wonderfully satisfying thing to do.*

*At age 86, I work for a wonderful company, which appreciates the money made from a magazine I edited for many years and so they let me continue to have a job and get paid.*

*Repeat: the work doesn't have to be so-called important or attention grabbing, just something you do well that helps other people, brings satisfaction and self respect to <u>you</u> and brings in a little money…enough to live on or <u>more</u>!"*

*—Helen Gurley Brown*

# Adriane M. Brown

## President and CEO, Honeywell Transportation Systems, USA

ADRIANE BROWN's 28 year ascent to the role of President and CEO of Honeywell Transportation Systems traces back to her early life in Richmond, Virginia.

Adriane's father was a schoolteacher and her mother, a school bus driver who later became a teacher's aid. They were steadfast in their Christian beliefs and commitment to education. Despite the conditions of a segregated Virginia, they expected a better world for Adriane and her big brother, Morris.

One significant event in their lives occurred in 1966 when she and her brother were headed to the third and sixth grades. Virginia had passed a law that required schools to be open to integration that year, and that all schools must integrate by 1967. Mildred and Andrew McClenny chose not to wait. They sent their two children, Morris and Adriane, along with three others from the neighborhood, to the integrated Bellwood Elementary School. It was a challenging year for Adriane and her four fellow trailblazers, but despite the trials and tribulations, they persevered. And perhaps 1967 went just a bit better for all because of the prior years' experiences.

What is perhaps a great example of progress was Adriane being elected class president in the 6th grade. She never looked back at the tearful pleas to her parents in 1966, to not send her to the "white" school. She quickly realized that she had to stand strong because failure was not an option. She was expected to live by the golden rule and though it would not be easy, she had to hold her head high and expect that same respect from others. This early life lesson reinforced that one will be faced with uncomfortable situations, but it is possible to take them on and reach a positive outcome.

After receiving a B.S. Degree in Environmental Health, Adriane was not sure what she wanted to be. She followed a path to Corning Glass Works, as a shift supervisor in an electronics manufacturing plant, a role at which she excelled. At 22 years old Adriane had found her stride.

She had always loved the business environment and after working for 10 years, she took a one year leave and pursued an MBA at Massachusetts Institute of Technology. She returned to Corning to continue her climb up the corporate ladder, reaching the role of Vice President & General Manager of a global business, leading the world's largest manufacturer of the device that removes pollution from a car's exhaust.

In 1999 Adriane took another leap of faith when she joined Honeywell's Aerospace division, where she was in charge of a $400M business and eventually a $1.3B business. By 2005 she returned to autos, becoming the President and CEO of Honeywell Transportation Systems, a $5B global business unit whose largest product line, turbochargers, reduce emissions and improve fuel economy on vehicles from around the world.

Adriane has been recognized for her trailblazing status including being named to the Automotive News' list of 100 leading women in the North American automotive industry and in Fortune Magazines' Women to Watch, in 2005 and 2006 respectively. She is a member of the Executive Leadership Council and she serves on the Board of Directors of Jobs for American's Graduates, the leading US drop-out prevention program.

Her career path is one that would have been difficult to plan but has served her well. From manufacturing to sales and marketing to general management, it has always been about inspiring those around her to take on tough goals and to enjoy the path to not only achieving those goals but exceeding them. It's always been about people, and the principles her parents inspired so deeply.

It is Adriane's hope that she and her husband continue the legacy of promise in the world in their daughter who says she wants to be a CEO when she grows up!

*"I used to hate the word 'ambition' because in my mind, I saw it as Blind Ambition. I came to realize that ambition means being willing to step outside of your comfort zone. It means taking a leap of faith, stepping up to a challenge, and living your values. So, with integrity, be ambitious! Raise the bar and deliver more than others think is possible!"*
—Adriane M. Brown

# Jayne-Anne Gadhia

## CEO, Virgin Money, England

When recounting the career progression of JAYNE-ANNE GADHIA, the first thing people seem to recall is that her career was inspired by an article she read in the U.K. celebrity magazine "Hello." Truth is, she was already deeply immersed in an amazing career path long before she read that now famous article about Sir Richard Branson on the train.

Jayne-Anne Gadhia was born in the West Midlands of England and was raised in the town of Norfolk. A defining moment for the young Jayne-Anne was when she became one of a group of seventeen girls who were the first to be admitted into what was until then, an all-boys school. She attributes this experience as having created her ability to survive in a man's world.

After completing university Jayne-Anne began training for her career as a chartered accountant. Three years later, upon certification, she took a position with a financial company, Norwich Union. In typical Gadhia fashion she equates her first big break with a crisis, namely the stock market collapse of 1987 in the U.K. Although she had no related experience, she was persuaded to accept the position of director of marketing. Under her leadership, within 12 months sales rose 300%! Another crisis, this time internal to the company propelled Jayne-Anne into the spotlight again. It was her task to regain the confidence of regulatory agencies and investors after the company was embroiled in a "mis-selling" scandal. Once again she prevailed.

Shortly thereafter Jayne-Anne took that legendary ride on the train. While reading about the brilliant businessman who was the force behind the Virgin empire, she speculated about what it would be like to work with someone as dynamic and passionate as Sir Richard Branson. As fate would have it, a friend introduced her to the person who was tasked with setting up a Virgin financial company and that was the beginning of Jayne-Anne's stunning career with Virgin Direct.

When Virgin Direct was sold to the Bank of Scotland, Jayne-Anne remained with the company. She rose to become the head of consumer finance, in charge of the mortgage division worth 67 billion pounds (approximately $118 Billion US Dollars).

Recently, she returned to work for Sir Richard Branson and her reasons were clear. It was not only that she admired and respected his business acumen and ethics, she needed to know that the long hours spent away from her daughter and husband were worthwhile.

As head of Virgin Money, Jayne-Anne undertook the challenge of saving a famous but floundering British bank, Northern Rock, something that the Bank of England and a raft of high ranking executives could not manage to do.

If one thing is certain, it is that Jayne-Anne Gadhia has an extraordinary gift for creating order out of mayhem. She is driven to make a positive difference and sums up her motivation by stating that she didn't want to reach the age of 60 only to find her career had been comprised of nothing more than a series of dull insurance jobs. No chance of that!

Courtesy of Jayne-Anne Gadhia

*"Many years ago when I was going through a difficult time I was talking to someone who mentored both me and Stella Rimmington.\**

*I asked him how on earth she (Stella) coped with everything thrown at her. He said they had discussed that only the previous day.*

*She said that she knew that all the problems thrown at her would be thrown at whoever sat in the same chair—they are issues that go with the territory and not personally directed.*

*'Don't take it personally' has been the mantra I have lived by at work ever since—and it has been invaluable in keeping me sane, focused and relatively level headed!*

*Thanks Stella!"*

—Jayne-Anne Gadhia

* Stella Rimmington is the former Director General of Britain's MI5 and the first women to hold this position. She is now a successful writer of "thriller" fiction

19

# Susan M. Ivey

## President and CEO, Reynolds America, USA

SUSAN M. IVEY did not start her professional career with aspirations to be one of the most powerful women in the world and only one of a handful of female CEOs of a Fortune 500 company. In fact, she worked her way through high school in a real estate office, filing listings.

After attending the University of Florida where she obtained her Bachelor of Science/Business degree in 1980, her first job was selling office equipment, a job she thoroughly disliked. She then was offered an opportunity at Brown & Williamson (B&W) Tobacco in 1981 where she became a sales representative. The sales force was very under-represented by women at that time and Susan tried to be "one of the guys." As her career advanced at the company and she found herself sitting in meetings overseas, Susan found that there were even fewer women. The first time it truly struck her that she was the only woman at a meeting was when she went to the women's restroom and realized she was the only one in there.

During her time at B&W (a subsidiary of British American Tobacco), she took on ever more challenging roles while completing her Masters in Business Administration in 1987. Susan eventually became the President and CEO of the company in 2001. With the merger of British American with Reynolds Tobacco in July of 2004, opportunities emerged for Susan, which she took up with her usual enthusiasm. In July 2006 she became the Chair, President and CEO of Reynold's American, which employs over 7000 people.

Her role is not one for the faint of heart. Her firm has a product, which particularly in the US, has dealt with years of litigation. Now Susan's mandate is to make the firm profitable and restore its reputation.

She sees her role as a steward of the shareholders and works at building a constructive dialogue with all stakeholders, including the anti-tobacco lobby. Susan believes that by having an effective communication channel you can develop ideas and approaches that are both better for business and better for society. Susan has always been a strong advocate and voice for women in business, and the senior leadership at Reynolds reflects this—half of the team is comprised of women. She serves on the Women's Leadership Initiative for the United Way of America. She also serves on the Board of Advisors for Women in Business and Economics at Salem College.

In a speech to a graduating class at the University of Florida Susan stated her 7 Keys to Success which are:

> *"Who you are is a lot more important that what you know; Meet and greet people on your street; Every so often you need to be scared; Learn from your mentors, and learn from your TORmentors; Sometimes you need to be like a Golden Retriever (have fun); Sometimes you need to be a Jack Russell terrier (leaping at opportunity); Get your priorities right."*

Yet what is success to Susan? "The legacy that you leave behind you in this world is the difference you make in countless lives and careers whose paths cross your own. That is your best shot at immortality. How will the business world—or your personal world—be different because you were here? If people can't imagine where they'd be without you, then you know the meaning of success."

Courtesy of Reynolds America

*"Be passionate—<u>love</u> what you do! We spend more time at work than anywhere else. It is <u>essential</u> to your success, fulfillment, and happiness that you enjoy your colleagues and are passionate about what you do."*
—Susan M. Ivey

# Suzanne Nora Johnson

## Former Vice Chairman, Senior Director, Goldman Sachs, USA

When one encounters descriptions of SUZANNE NORA JOHNSON, the words which are used most often are inclusive, supportive and a team player. Those descriptors seem all the more remarkable when one realizes that Suzanne Nora Johnson is one of only a hand full of women in the world who has made it to the top of what has rightly been portrayed as one of the most competitive and cut-throat of fields—investment banking. Furthermore she did so in the single most successful securities firm in the history of New York's fabled Wall Street—Goldman Sachs.

Suzanne Nora Johnson has impeccable credentials. Born in Chicago (her father was a doctor and her mother a housewife), Suzanne was one of five children. She earned a BA from the University of Southern California and a law degree from Harvard. Suzanne began work as a law clerk on the U.S. Court of Appeals and subsequently joined a prestigious law firm, Simpson, Thacher & Bartlett. In 1985 she joined Goldman Sachs Group and seven years later was made a partner. By 2004 Suzanne Nora Johnson was promoted to the position of Vice Chairman of Goldman Sachs. Suzanne retired from her position as Vice Chairman, Goldman Sachs in 2007 but continues to serve as a Senior Director for the company.

She has a highly developed social conscience which results in her being a tireless contributor to many worthwhile causes. Suzanne sits as a director on numerous boards including AIG Inc., Intuit Inc., Pfizer Inc. and Visa Inc. and on many not-for-profit boards such as the American Red Cross, Brookings Institution, Carnegie Institution of Washington, the Council for Excellence in Government, TechnoServe and Women's World Banking.

Suzanne is a committed supporter of the notion that women should be able to rise as high in their chosen fields as their talents and dedication will permit. She has expressed her belief that as a gender, women generally tend not to self-promote and that there are many women who are actually at the top of their professions but who are not widely recognized.

Suzanne Nora Johnson is a person who has been able to remain true to her principals and who has retained her focus in the face of immense competition. She once attributed the success of Goldman Sachs to its ability to attract and retain employees who were both driven individualists and collaborative team players.

Certainly Suzanne Nora Johnson has proven herself to be the epitome of such a description.

Courtesy of Suzanne Nora Johnson

*"Be generous of spirit—even in adversity and when under assault."*
—Suzanne Nora Johnson

# Kiran Mazumdar-Shaw

## Chair Biocon, Entrepreneur, Scientist, India

She has been called India's Biotech Queen, but when KIRAN MAZUMDAR-SHAW was trying to establish her business, she probably felt more like a pinball being hurled from obstacle to obstacle. The thought of not succeeding didn't enter her thoughts. Today she is recognized as one of India's top businesswomen, as well as the wealthiest.

She is the daughter of a brewmaster and a stay-at-home mother. Her family was progressive and instead of arranging a marriage for Kiran, they encouraged her to pursue an education. Her first degree was from the University of Bangalore in Zoology. She followed this by qualifying as a Master Brewer from Ballarat University in Australia in 1975, India's first woman to achieve this standing.

Upon her return to India she expected to be fending off job offers, but instead found that no one would hire her. Kiran found herself being told that the job was too rough for a woman.

She consulted for two years and then was approached by the then owner of Biocon Biochemicals, at the time an Irish specialty chemicals company that was trying to break into the Indian market. The owner of Biocon saw Kiran as an ideal partner. So in 1978, Biocon India started out with $10,000 and a plan to produce enzymes for beer, wine, paper, animal feed and detergents.

Kiran would have happily embraced a glass ceiling, because what she ran into was one made of steel. It took her weeks to just find office space to rent because the landlords thought that she wouldn't be "good" for the rent. She also had difficulty finding anyone who would work for her and eventually was able to get a family friend to fill in as a secretary. Kiran was finally able to get a small line of credit for the enterprise, after a chance meeting with a banker at a friend's wedding. Next the raw materials vendors insisted that a male manager accompany her if she wanted to buy their goods, as the presence of the male manager provided her with credibility.

Under Kiran's stewardship, Biocon has evolved from its inception as an industrial enzymes company to a fully integrated bio-pharmaceutical enterprise, and is one of the top 20 such firms in the world. But she has taken the company beyond being a star in generics and through Biocon's subsidiaries Syngene and Clinigene, provides contract research/manufacturing and clinical research, respectively. She was awarded an honorary Doctorate of Science from Ballarat University in recognition of her pre-eminent contributions to the field of biotechnology.

Kiran was recently recognized by Forbes magazine as one of the "Top 100 Most Powerful Women" in the world. She has also been acknowledged for giving back to her community. Kiran is passionate about helping those less fortunate and donates half of the firm's dividends to fund hospitals and to provide health insurance for poor villagers. As such, she was awarded the Padma Bhushan, one of India's highest civilian honors.

Kiran is always looking to the horizon and the next opportunity. New things electrify her imagination, so don't expect her to slow down anytime soon.

And next time you are in a bookstore, you might want to pick up a copy of Kiran's coffee table book *Ale and Arty* a fusion of beer facts and paintings that accompany each chapter. In it you'll find anything you've ever wanted to know about beer and brewing!

Courtesy of Kiran Mazumdar-Shaw

*"Take on challenges with a sense of purpose. Success comes to those who own problems, not tasks. Solving problems generates a tremendous sense of confidence and satisfaction. It is this approach that has helped me become a successful entrepreneur. This problem solving ethos is strongly engrained in our HR practices. I truly believe that this approach can make ordinary people do extra-ordinary things."*
—Kiran Mazumdar-Shaw

# Blossom O'Meally Nelson

## Business Executive, Educator, Environmentalist, Jamaica

Many have heard of the Jamaican Bobsled team and it was BLOSSOM O'MEALLY-NELSON's two sons who pioneered the sport in Jamaica. Of course with a mother who is a pioneer, it is no surprise that her children would reach for the improbable and succeed.

Blossom has the distinction of having been the first female Postmaster General of Jamaica. During her six years in this role she established the Postal Corporation of Jamaica for the commercialization and modernization of the Post. She followed that with being the Pro-Chancellor and Chairman of Council for the University of Technology in Jamaica for 17 years, which allowed her to focus on her passion for education (her postgraduate studies and PhD are in education). She has now turned to the private sector and is Chief Operating Officer for Aeromar Logistics, Jamaica's foremost Third Party Logistics provider.

Blossom is a dynamic speaker and never fails to impress audiences with her insight, mingled with a wonderful sense of humor. She is the author of the book *Hazards of Entrepreneurship* and at one time hosted a television program called "Businessline." Her entrepreneurship is evident as owner of Decorator's Dream, a boutique store for paint and paint accessories and she also markets her human resource development products under the brand name Personal Excellence Unlimited.

Before it was trendy to do so, Blossom was involved in the environmental movement. She was a founding Director of the Environmental Foundation of Jamaica and for eleven years chaired the Jamaica Conservation and Development Trust.

It is no wonder that she has recently received national honors by way of the Order of Distinction, Commander Class, for outstanding public service. This follows on the heels of other awards such as the prestigious Woman of Excellence award from the Kiwanis Club of New Kingston and she has been honored as a Woman of Great Esteem by the Q-Kingdom Ministries of New York.

As Annual Guest Lecturer 2007 to the Jamaican Women's Political Caucus Blossom said: "Celebrate womanhood—the complexity of it makes life an adventure, not so much an external adventure in climbing physical mountains and swimming literal rivers, but in climbing the mountains of our own fears and swimming the rivers of our own tears experiencing that internal adventure to its fullest."

Blossom has made service her guiding principle—which also extends beyond people. She owns dogs, birds and a macaw and is known for picking up stray dogs and taking them to the Jamaican Society for the Prevention of Cruelty to Animals in an effort to give them a chance.

And if you are down in Jamaica sometime, try to catch Blossom's stand-up comedy routine at the annual "Powerful Women Perform for Charity" evening!

*"Understand that, as a woman, the most significant thing that you can do in life is to find your own purpose. Having found that purpose, your mission is to pursue it with all the passion and courage that you can find within yourself. You are not alone as women everywhere grow in resolve towards the common purpose of freedom and equity for women across the globe, and you will find that the whole universe celebrates your sound and will make way for your success!"*
—Blossom O'Meally-Nelson

# Heather Reisman

## CEO and Founder, Indigo Books & Music, Canada

HEATHER REISMAN is often referred to as Canada's "Chief Booklover" which is appropriate given her role as the head of the nation's largest book retailer. So it may be surprising that there is one word that is missing in Heather's vocabulary. That word is "can't."

Throughout her life, she has pursued her interests with determined passion and these have now melded into an aria—merging her love of books, music and business.

After attending McGill University in Montreal, she began her career working as a caseworker. Soon however, the world of business caught her attention. She was given an opportunity to work at Intergroupe, an innovative consulting firm in Montreal where she met and worked with one of the pioneering consultants in the field of strategy and change. This led a few years later to her co-founding Paradigm Consulting. Paradigm was the world's first strategic change consultancy. It pioneered organizational change strategies still used in corporations today.

In 1992 she became President of Cott Corporation, which at the time was a small, Canadian-based regional bottler. During her tenure as President, Cott grew to become the world's largest retailer-branded beverage suppliers. Harvard University wrote two case studies on Cott's growth providing students and other businesses with insight on what drove the phenomenal success.

Heather's passion for books and music were always part of her everyday life and finally, in 1996 she launched Indigo Books and Music. Conceived as the world's first booklovers' cultural department store, Indigo was the first book retail chain to add gifts and their own cafes to their distinctive store locations, thereby transforming the retail shopping experience. Booklover events are now standard fare throughout the Indigo chain.

In 2001, Indigo merged with what was then the largest book retailer in Canada, Chapters. At the time both firms were reporting large annual losses and the amalgamation of the two conglomerates was seen as the only way to salvage the bookstore industry in Canada. Overcoming the hurdles and the naysayers, Heather transformed Indigo into a successful enterprise that is now synonymous with the joy of reading in Canada and business success.

Indigo Inc. has launched a new chain of stores called "Pistachio" which carry eco-friendly gifts, paper and beauty products. Opening first in Toronto, the expectation is to expand across North America. And with Heather's uncanny ability to be ahead of the curve in determining market needs, you know that Pistachio will be extremely successful.

She is the recipient of many awards which include several for her entrepreneurship, as well as an Honorary Doctorate from Ryerson University. Heather is also on the board of several major corporations.

Through Indigo, Heather has also created the Love of Reading Foundation, which provides books to high-needs elementary schools in Canada. Since its inception, the Indigo Love of Reading Foundation has raised over $6.0 million and provided support to 48 schools across Canada.

Heather Reisman is not only a business visionary, she is also a true philanthropist in both word and deed.

*"Believe in yourself and your aspirations. Don't let doubts or naysayers stop you from reaching your dreams. The only difference between those who do, and those who don't is that those who do—do!"*
—Heather Reisman

Courtesy of Heather Reisman

# Genevieve Thiers

## CEO Sittercity, Opera Singer, USA

Learning about GENEVIEVE THIERS is akin to following the lives and careers of at least two or three different people—and old people at that! At first glance it is inconceivable that one woman, no more than thirty years of age, could have already packed so much into life.

While studying music and english as an undergraduate at Boston College, Genevieve generated income by baby-sitting for more than 30 families. It was a natural activity for her, as she and her twin sister had run a baby-sitting operation during their high school years in Philadelphia.

While a senior at Boston College, Genevieve conceived the concept of a website which matched baby-sitters with parents, much like some of the familiar on-line dating sites. After graduation, during her time working full-time for IBM, she developed a business plan for the website.

She founded Sittercity.com in 2001. It was the internet's first and largest website dedicated to providing secure, reliable access to local caregivers. From its humble beginnings—Genevieve reportedly had to borrow the $120 to buy the domain name and to print the initial 20,000 fliers—to a corporation which has 30 full-time employees and more than a million caregiver profiles nationwide. The growth of Sittercity can only be described as phenomenal. Her success resulted in featured articles in the New York Times and interviews on the Today Show and others. Her first book, *Love at First Sit*, was published in 2008.

In 2002 Genevieve moved the company to Chicago, as she had decided to pursue her passion for opera and had enrolled in Northwestern University's School of Music's Opera Performance Masters program. It was this act which truly put Genevieve into a class by herself. How? By exercising her extraordinary entrepreneurial skills in her company and simultaneously excelling in her studies while spending evenings practicing and performing opera.

And the story continues. In 2004, after graduating from the Master's program, Genevieve assessed the situation and decided that spending the ensuing

5 to 10 years paying her dues, while waiting to be awarded her first role as a professional opera singer, was not her style.

So with customary energy and drive she and a friend founded their own opera production company—OperaModa (www.operamoda.com), thereby sending a clear message to the opera community that things can and should change. The mission of OperaModa was not only to cast and hire young performers, it was to get the message across that opera—especially America opera—is still relevant in today's society.

Although Genevieve describes herself as a highly ambitious person, she has demonstrated that she is so much more. She is a person who has discovered the way to make *all* her dreams a reality.

*"Don't believe anyone that tells you that you can't excel at two things at once. I've followed two passions in my life and have had twice the happiness."*
—Genevieve Thiers

# Joanne Thomas Yaccato

## Entrepreneur, Author, Women's Advocate, Canada

JOANNE THOMAS YACCATO is the President and Founder of The Thomas Yaccato Group, a consulting firm known as Corporate Canada's Gender Lens. This firm specializes in helping companies create a critically important gender lens that they need in order to create authentic products, services and business strategies to attract the attention and loyalty of women consumers.

Her ground-breaking book *The 80% Minority: Reaching the Real World of Women Consumers* was the first book in Canada to offer the truth behind women consumers and their relationship with corporations. In fact, studies showed that 80% of every consumer dollar spent in Canada was controlled directly or indirectly by women and yet women felt wholly unacknowledged. Joanne's work has proven that there is a straight-line connection between getting it right with women and getting it right with everyone else, thereby positively affecting a corporation's bottom-line. Her newest book *The Gender Intelligent Retailer: Discover the Connection Between Women Consumers and Business Growth*, takes her innovative "gender lens" approach to the world of retailing.

Yet it is more than just her knowledge and understanding which makes her so effective—it is her unfailing sense of humor. A business article written by Joanne entitled, *What Women (really) Want* with the by-line "Hint: It's not that 'gotta be a thin, beautiful, married, mother and corporate executive in order to be taken seriously crap'" encapsulates her approach. While the article goes on to make serious and compelling points, it is her extraordinary ability to communicate her concepts in a memorable way which has been the underpinning of her sustained success. Women consumers and corporations have profited equally from Joanne's constructive approach.

Her bestselling books are written in the same fashion, using her personal experience and hilarious misadventures to convey her ideas. One of these books, the newly-released 10th Anniversary Edition of *Balancing Act: A Canadian Woman's Financial Success Guide and Raising Your Business: A Canadian*

*Woman's Guide to Entrepreneurship*, was nominated for the prestigious National Business Book Award.

Joanne is a regular contributor to Canada's media including CBC, CTV and the country's top financial press and national newspapers. She has been nominated for the Governor General's award, and has received two nominations each for the Ernst & Young's Entrepreneur of the Year Award and the YWCA's National Women of Distinction Award.

She has recently been a consultant to the International Finance Corporation, a World Bank subsidiary, which will distribute millions of dollars in international funds to Africa. Her goal is to help African banks understand the power of women entrepreneurs—providing them the money and self-assurance they need to grow their businesses, and therefore helping the impoverished continent to achieve sustainable economic security.

And with Joanne's drive and commitment she is bound to help make this happen.

Courtesy of Joanne Thomas Yaccato

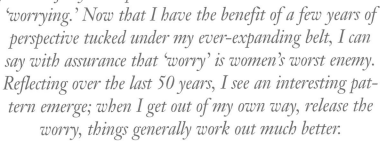

*"As I found out this year, there is nothing quite like turning 50 to propel 'philosopher' to the top of your resume. Now that I'm a card carrying member of the 'sage and wise' club, I shake my head at the staggering amount of time and energy—two of my most precious resources—that I wasted on 'worrying.' Now that I have the benefit of a few years of perspective tucked under my ever-expanding belt, I can say with assurance that 'worry' is women's worst enemy. Reflecting over the last 50 years, I see an interesting pattern emerge; when I get out of my own way, release the worry, things generally work out much better.*

*As Mark Twain once astutely remarked, 'I am an old man and have known a great many troubles, but most of them never happened.' Don't' wait until you're 50 to finally put worry in its proper place; six feet under the compost pile."*

—Joanne Thomas Yaccato

Ann Tottenham
*Canada*

Alison Elliot
*Scotland*

Baroness
Neuberger
*England*

# Enriching the Soul

In the span of human history women have always participated in the religious community. However women have been accepted into leadership roles in these institutions for what one can consider a comparative "blink of an eye." Slowly, but steadily, over the last couple of decades, some of these traditionally patriarchal organizations have allowed women to lead, recognizing their positive contribution to enriching the souls of humanity.

None of the women in this segment expected to be trailblazers in the world of religion. In fact, when they began their journeys, leading in their religious orders was not an option. Yet, leading the way is what they have done by demonstrating to women that there is a world of opportunity awaiting them within religious establishments.

# Alison Elliot, OBE

## Former Moderator, Church of Scotland, Scotland

When Dr. ALISON ELLIOT was elected for a one year term, as Moderator of the General Assembly of The Church of Scotland in 2004, she was the first woman to ever hold this position and the first non-minister since the 16th century.

Like many women doing a new thing, Alison would prefer to be remembered for her achievements as a human being, not as a woman. However, her gender is mentioned in each introduction, from church chancels and AIDS hospice steps, to European political and church council lecterns. She is the embodiment of the profound changes in her church.*

The Church of Scotland only consented to ministerial ordination for women in 1968, one year after a group of six women made a ground-breaking appeal to the General Assembly for them to be allowed to be fully ordained. This meant not just eldership and being licensed to preach the word, but to the ministry of word and sacraments. This was only two years after women were permitted to be ordained to eldership. These women and others like Dr. Elliot have enabled the splintering of the clerical glass ceiling.

Alison was born in Edinburgh in 1948 and educated at Bathgate Academy and Edinburgh University, where she gained an MA in Mathematics with General Linguistics. She then moved on to the University of Sussex where she graduated with a Master's of Science in Experimental Psychology. Alison subsequently obtained her PhD in children's language development from Edinburgh University.

Since 2001, Alison has been the Associate Director of Edinburgh's University Centre for Theology and Public Issues. She has also represented her church on many ecumenical and civic bodies. She is on the governing body of

---

* From the Presbyterian Record, April 1, 2005

the Conference of European Churches and chairs the Lay Advisory Group for the Royal College of Physicians of Edinburgh. She has taken part in working groups on health, criminal justice, asylum policy, constitutional matters and land reform. In 2003 she was awarded the Officer of The British Empire designation for her services to the Church of Scotland and ecumenical relations.

Alison was once quoted as saying "To be human is to be constantly changing. If we are not experiencing change we're probably dead….However change seems to come out of nowhere. But yet, though unseen and unrecognized, growth and change continue, the pressures for change build and suddenly something like a switch goes on and a whole series of changes are triggered."*

Alison is one of those who have helped the switch go on so that a whole cluster of positive changes could happen.

Courtesy of Alison Elliot

*"Throw yourself completely into the task that's to hand and possibilities will emerge that you could never have imagined."*
—Dr. Alison Elliot

37

# Baroness Julia Neuberger

## Rabbi, Author, Social Reformer, England

JULIA NEUBERGER was Britain's second female Rabbi and the first to have her own synagogue. This was not her planned career, but as Julia has stated, most things that have happened in her life have happened by accident.

She actually began her studies at Cambridge in Assyriology (the archaeological, historical, and linguistic study of ancient Mesopotamia). Julia's interest in this area was spawned when, as a child, she played in the British Museum and became absolutely fascinated by the Assyrians. Cambridge required that she also have a subsidiary subject so she chose Hebrew. Her pursuit of Assyriology was thwarted by a few external political factors when in the late 1960's she was refused entry to Iraq because she was Jewish. The following year, she planned to go on an archeological dig in Turkey, but the British were banned from digging in Turkey. So Julia changed to Hebrew for her primary subject.

When a professor at the university first floated the idea to Julia that she should consider becoming a Rabbi, her first reaction was, "Don't be ridiculous! Women aren't Rabbis and I'm not that religious!"[*]

Yet her professor insisted, noting that being a Rabbi is about being a teacher of Judaism and as Julia later discovered on her own, her faith was stronger than she had recognized. He arranged for Julia to attend Leo Baeck College, first for only a day a week in her fourth year of university and then full time. Julia was only one of a few women studying Judaism. In 1977 she became a Rabbi and served the South London Liberal Synagogue for twelve years.

She has always been involved in politics and matters of social conscience, which is not surprising given that she grew up in a family where healthy debate was encouraged. Julia has always thought it worthwhile to question the status quo.

---

[*] Thursday 8 April 2004 on BBC Radio 3—Interview with Julia Neuberger

Julia is passionate about issues surrounding healthcare, including the status of public health, caring for dying people, healthcare ethics and treatment of the elderly. She was able to pursue her interest in these topics through positions at healthcare related institutions including Harvard Medical School and as Chief Executive of an independent health charity. She is currently chairing the Commission on the Future of Volunteering and has recently been appointed the Prime Minister's Champion for Volunteering. She was installed as a Life Peer in 2004, in recognition of her phenomenal achievements.

Julia has authored several books on a variety of subjects including Judaism, women, healthcare ethics and on caring for dying people. All her books are incredibly thought provoking such as her latest book *Not Dead Yet—a Manifesto for Old Age*, which has garnered quite a bit of heated discussion on the treatment of the elderly and their expectations.

But then Julia always welcomes passionate debate!

Courtesy of Derek Tamea

*"Never act when angry—*
*always wait till you've cooled down."*
—Baroness Julia Neuberger

# The Right Reverend Ann Tottenham

## Anglican Church Bishop, Canada

After being elected as Bishop by the Anglican Church in 1997, ANN TOTTENHAM was asked whether she always aspired to being a Bishop.

"I roared with laughter," says Bishop Ann. "Women have only had the opportunity to become bishops since the early '90's, so it was not something that I gave any thought to while growing up." So for Bishop Ann, life has been a series of wonderful surprises.

Her father was the Headmaster of the junior division of a boys' school, which is where Bishop Ann grew up along with her 3 brothers, and her mother who worked in the school library and her father's office.

When she graduated from university in 1962, she enrolled in a theology program which prepared men for ordination and graduated with a Bachelor of Sacred Theology in 1965.

There were not a huge number of career choices in the church for women and Ann always wanted to be a teacher so for a period of time this is what she did.

But Ann felt that she wanted to do something more and she always had a lot of questions about God. Ordination for women was not an option at the time, so she joined the Anglican Church as a nun and was part of the order for three and a half years in the late 1960's. She considers her time at the convent an eye-opening experience, working in the inner city of Atlantic City, New Jersey, marching in the Anti-Vietnam protests and working for the betterment of society. "It certainly wasn't what some people perceive to be a quiet and sedate nun's life!"

When Ann left she returned to teaching, always with schools that had a religious orientation. She became Headmistress of Bishop Strachan School in Toronto, a position she held for 14 years. During this time she became a deacon and subsequently, in 1983 a priest in the Anglican Church. Then in 1997 she was ordained as Suffragan Bishop of Toronto,—at the time only one of 10 women bishops globally, and the second in Canada—a role she retired from in 2005. She continues with a ministry of teaching and preaching as it would be difficult for someone with Bishop Ann's energy to totally retire.

Bishop Ann had strong female role models along the way, having attended a girls' high school "A female school, led by women." Her grandmother, and her mother also provided great inspiration. "I recognize now the influence these women had in my formative years, but I didn't realize it at the time."

Early in her career, Bishop Ann was criticized as not being active enough in women's issues, but she notes she prefers to "lead by example, as opposed to marching and shouting."

Although there are still fewer than 30 women Bishops globally in the Anglican Church, the growth since the early '90's has been exponential, probably a result of women like Bishop Ann who are "leading by example."

Courtesy of Bishop Ann Tottenham

*"Decide what your priorities are. If your first priority is to promote women's rights, you need to act on that and realize that this will probably have consequences for your career. If your first priority is your career, you will promote women's rights by who you are and by what you do in that career. In this case, being a shining example in a leadership role is the best thing you can do to forward the cause of women in today's world."*
—Bishop Ann Tottenham

Karen
Kain
*Canada*

Pamela Wallin
*Canada*

Dame Evelyn
Glennie
*England*

Deepa
Mehta
*Canada*

Della Reese
*USA*

# Spotlight

Barbara Dennerlein
*Germany*

Miriam Němcová
*Czech Republic*

Anna Jokai
*Hungary*

Evelyne Aiello
*France*

The world of entertainment casts a broad net across a virtually endless number of possibilities. Because we see women in various roles in movies and television, listen to female singers and musicians, read books by women authors, watch female dancers, as well as have news delivered via women at the anchor desks—our tendency would be to believe that this is not a category that would warrant the moniker of "trailblazer."

The reality is that the world of entertainment and the media is a reflection of other portions of society and it is a sector where women have, and continue to, experience impediments to advancement. Nonetheless these barriers proved to be no match for the women in the "Spotlight."

# Evelyne Aiello

## Conductor, France

EVELYNE AIELLO has been hailed as "one of the biggest hopes of the young generation of conductors of French orchestras. She possesses a transmission gift that cannot be learned and that identifies the true interpreter of music."*

Being a conductor of an orchestra is still a relative rarity among women. In fact in some of the largest philharmonic orchestras in Europe, it has only been in the last decade that women were accepted as full-time member musicians. So for Evelyne to have achieved the status of conductor is certainly a tribute to her talent and resolve.

She studied at several renowned schools of music in Europe including the Ecole Normale de Musique de Paris, Conservatoire Nationale Supérieur de Musique de Paris, the Academy Chigiana in Italy, and the Mozarteum in Salzburg Austria. Evelyne honed her conducting skills under the tutelage of a number of noted European conductors including Franco Ferrara (Italy), Ferdinand Leitner (Germany) and the Swiss composer Rolf Liebermann.

Over the last 20 years Evelyne has been conducting numerous professional and student orchestras in Europe and abroad. These include conducting for numerous French orchestras, the Hungarian Radio Orchestra, New Boston Orchestra and others too numerous to mention.

Evelyne is known for exploring symphonic music beyond its standard boundaries. She can provide her audience with a customary repertoire of symphonic classics, but will also conduct performances with contemporary music and lyrics. Evelyne had the opportunity to work with such famed ballet dancers as Rudolf Nureyev and Patrick Dupont while conducting the Ballet de l'Opera de Paris.

* Marcel Landowski (1915-1999) French composer from http://polymusie.free.fr/aiellog.htm

The classical music world is in its own renaissance and is beginning to recognize women as equals both in the "pit" and on the "podium." Fortunately women such as Evelyne are leading the way, demonstrating that true talent knows no gender.

*"Don't listen to any advice that will stop you
from following your dreams."*
—Evelyne Aiello

# Barbara Dennerlein

## Jazz Organist, Composer & Arranger, Germany

BARBARA DENNERLEIN is an internationally celebrated Hammond B3 organ virtuoso. Audiences are captivated by her talent, her absolute mastery of the instrument, her taste and not least, her warm personality. It is as if the instrument she plays is a seamless extension of herself—passionate and full of life. She understands better than anyone how to use her instrument to the fullest, creating a sound and a musical style that is unmistakably her own. Her brilliant technique has breathed new life into the venerable Hammond organ, an instrument long neglected in modern jazz.

Born in Munich, Germany in 1964, she fell in love with the sound of the organ at an early age. She was only eleven when a home organ became part of the Dennerlein household. Her father, himself an organ fan, admitted that he acted a bit out of self-interest when he bought the organ as a Christmas present. If Barbara lost interest, he could always play it himself. Yet that didn't happen, as Barbara never took her hands off the instrument again. While others in her age group were strumming *All You Need is Love* on the guitar, Barbara remained fascinated by the sound of the organ.

And so began Barbara's own journey of discovery into the world of music. In addition to studying the classical repertoire of standards, she began to compose her own music at an early age. Following her first performance as a thirteen year-old, she began to play in clubs regularly at the age of fifteen. By the early 1980's she was already an internationally celebrated jazz performer, with her music having been released on several prestigious record labels. Barbara also established her own label, Bebab Records and has recorded numerous CDs over the years on this label as well.

It is an awe-inspiring experience to watch Barbara live on stage. As the most important and successful German jazz export, she is familiar with large international festival stages and intimate clubs alike. The list of venues where she has astounded audiences is as varied as it is long and includes "The

Bluenote" clubs in New York City and Tokyo, the "Ronnie Scott's Club" and the "Jazz Café" in London, as well as jazz festivals around the globe. Besides her nearly endless list of live performances, Barbara has made numerous appearances on international radio and television.

In 2004 Barbara gave musical expression to her innermost thoughts and aspirations and captured these on a strikingly original and very personal CD. *In a Silent Mood* is a revealing and fascinating insight into her musical personality. Barbara's music is known for its ability to take the listeners on a journey into diverse musical worlds, presenting them with enthralling soundscapes.

Barbara Dennerlein is in a class of her own; she is without question, the First Lady of the Hammond Organ.

Courtesy of Barbara Dennerlein

*"First of all, never forget that you are unique! Whatever your goal in life might be, it is always worthwhile. It is always worth fighting for your opinions and your personal freedom. Never doubt, just do it! There is something, a talent or a gift, which you have and nobody else possesses and it is your duty to discover it and to make it real. This will surely lead to a happy and fulfilling life."*
—Barbara Dennerlein

# Dame Evelyn Glennie

## Solo Percussionist, England

Dame EVELYN GLENNIE is the first person in musical history to successfully create and sustain a full time career as a solo percussionist. Evelyn gives more than 100 performances a year all over the world to universal critical acclaim. She has performed with virtually all of the world's finest orchestras and greatest conductors in some of the most famous concert halls.

She grew up on a farm north of Aberdeen, Scotland and credits her interest in music to the excellent music education she received at her primary school, where the students were fed a continuous diet of music from a visiting music teacher.

For the first ten years of her career virtually every performance she gave was in some way a first—the first time an orchestra had performed with a percussion soloist, the first solo percussion performance at a venue or festival, or the world premiere of a new piece. Her diversity of collaborations has included artists from Sting to the Mormon Tabernacle Choir.

Outside of actual performance, Evelyn Glennie is constantly exploring other areas of creativity. She has written a best selling autobiography, Good Vibrations, collaborated on a film called *Touch the Sound*, and presented two series of her own television programmes for the BBC. Evelyn also appears regularly on television across the world including The David Letterman Show, Sesame Street, and many more. She has her own range of jewelry, the designs of which are based on her influences as a solo percussionist.

When Evelyn was 8 years old she began to lose her hearing as a result of a neurological disorder. A few years later she was profoundly deaf. In her biographical information this is not mentioned because Evelyn wants the focus to be on her music, not on her deafness. As she says in "The Hearing Essay" on her website (www.evelyn.co.uk); "If the audience is instead only wondering how a deaf musician can play percussion then I have failed as a musician." She explains that she can hear/feel sounds through the vibrations. "Deafness does not mean that you can't hear, only that there is something wrong with the ears."

After 20 years in the music business she has begun teaching privately, which allows her to explore the art of teaching and the world of sound therapy as a means of communication.

Evelyn was awarded the Officer of the British Empire in 1993 and in 2007 this was extended to Dame Commander for her services to music. She has received approximately 80 international awards including a Grammy.

Evelyn is full of drive and enthusiasm, brimming with ideas to improve the experience and redefine the very format of live performance itself.

Courtesy of Richard Eccleston © Sabina

*"Be true to yourself."*
—Dame Evelyn Glennie

# Anna Jokai

## Author, Hungary

ANNA JOKAI always loved to write, but it wasn't until she was thirty-four that she decided to pursue writing as a career. Now, over 30 years, 20 books, and multiple awards later Anna is glad that she gave up her accounting and teaching jobs to become an author.

She was born in 1932 to a middle class family in Budapest, Hungary. Early on she worked as an accountant, but in 1957 she decided to go to the Eötvös Loránd University, where by 1961, she had earned her degree as a teacher of Hungarian literature and history.

While Anna taught school for many years, she always wrote in her spare time. Her experiences with school life and the lives of her students often provided her with inspiration. Although the part-time writing provided her with a creative release and some success, it soon became evident that if she truly wanted to be a writer, she couldn't do it on a part-time basis. So she left teaching, and followed her passion of writing full time.

Always a strong supporter of the writing profession, Anna served for three years as vice-president of the Hungarian Writers' Association and then a subsequent three years as its President.

She has written more than 20 books (novels, short stories, essays and poems) which have been published in several languages. Her artistic goal is a quest for valid answers to the eternal question of human existence, which she calls spiritual realism. A common feature in her work is the fight against human indifference.

Her books have won several awards including the Kossuth Prize, the Hungarian Heredity Prize, the Book of the Year Prize and the Prima Primissima Prize.

One of her most popular books, *Ne Féljetek (Fear Not)*, is reflective of the spiritual values that Anna pursues in her works, noting the need for people to confront the difficulties in their lives.

Reading Anna's works will ensure that one pauses and thinks about how we view the world. And that is exactly what she intended!

*"My advice to women is to develop strong will-power, self-knowledge and recognize the grace of God in what they do."*
*—Anna Jokai*

Courtesy of Anna Jokai

# Karen Kain

Artistic Director, National Ballet of Canada,
Former Prima Ballerina, Canada

When KAREN KAIN was six years old her mother enrolled her in ballet class, with the intention, as Karen put it, "to improve my posture." And although many claim that they saw her potential, it is unlikely that anyone would have predicted that Karen would one day become the most revered ballerina in Canadian history.

Born in the early nineteen fifties in Hamilton, Ontario, Canada, Karen was the eldest of four children. At the young age of 11 Karen made the difficult decision to leave her home and family and to take up residence at Canada's National Ballet School in Toronto. A scant seven years later, Karen realized her childhood dream and was accepted into the National Ballet of Canada.

Much like the beautiful, unforgettable ballets she performed, Karen's life was full of drama, heartache and intense joy. The progression from a child in a middle-class family to an internationally loved performer was not without its hardships and sacrifices. To begin with, the tuition fees and school expenses were considerable. Furthermore, Karen was frequently told that she was too tall (at 5'7") and weighed too much to ever become a serious dancer. Although she had a lifelong struggle to sustain the expected low body weight, through her unswerving sense of commitment, passion and creative energy she overcame her insecurities and displayed her extraordinary gifts. When only nineteen Karen got her big break—the title role of Swan Lake.

Partnered over the years with such greats as Rudolf Nureyev, the Russian ballet superstar, Karen performed in many memorable ballets including Romeo & Juliet, The Nutcracker and The Sleeping Beauty. Nureyev also had a large impact on Karen's career by obtaining invitations for her to dance with some of the greatest ballet companies across the globe, including The Bolshoi Ballet, London Festival Ballet, and the Vienna State Opera Ballet.

After 26 years as a principal dancer, Karen undertook a rapturously and emotionally received cross-country farewell tour with the National Ballet of Canada. She went on to become the Chair of the Canada Council for the Arts and shortly thereafter she took on the position of Artistic Director of the National Ballet of Canada, the ballet company to which she had dedicated her career and life. Karen was motivated to carry the message of the ballet to people from all backgrounds and walks of life. She has even published a children's book, *The Nutcracker*, based on the ballet.

Since her unrivaled debut performance, Karen has received numerous national and international awards, both for her work as a performer and as an advocate for the arts and cultural development. She was awarded the Companion of the Order of Canada and is a recipient of the Governor General's Performing Arts Award for Lifetime Achievement. Internationally she was the first Canadian to be honored with France's Cartier Lifetime Achievement Award and in 2001 was named an Offier of the Order of Arts and Letters by the French Government.

The name "Karen Kain" is synonymous with tireless perfection. Through her impact as a role model for younger dancers and by her invaluable efforts to strengthen the art of ballet, her selfless dedication continues to inspire generation after generation.

*"Life is short, try to savour every moment."*
—Karen Kain

# Deepa Mehta

## Director, Producer, Screenwriter, Canada & India

DEEPA MEHTA is arguably Canada's most internationally renowned woman filmmaker. Watching one of her films is like being invited on an unexpected cinematic journey through a rainbow of emotions. Most of Deepa's films are provocative and one particularly resulted in passions being stoked to such a crescendo that 2000 protesters stormed and destroyed one of her film sets and threatened Deepa's life.

Deepa Mehta grew up in India, watching hundreds of movies in her father's theaters. When Deepa was very young her father took her to the projectionist's area and she was allowed to touch the machine where she was shown "the film." When she was allowed to touch the bottom of the screen where somebody was moving, she was enthralled and thought "this is magic."

Surprisingly, she did not have an early interest in becoming a filmmaker and instead chose to study philosophy at the University of Delhi, eventually earning a master's degree in the subject. She had planned to continue in university and do her PhD dissertation when she met a friend who said they needed someone to work part-time at a place called the Cinematic Workshop, which made documentary films in Delhi. She learned to do sound, camera work, editing and then made her own documentary about a 15-year-old child bride who had worked in her family home. Deepa had discovered her passion.

She immigrated to Canada in 1973 and truly embarked on her cinematic career despite having no formal training in filmmaking. Her first feature film *Sam and Me* debuted in 1991, followed by the widely acclaimed movie *Camilla* in 1994, which starred Jessica Tandy and Bridget Fonda.

Recognizing the power of film to create dialogue, her next foray was with contentious subject matter and filmed in her native country of India. Her film trilogy *Fire*, *Earth* and *Water* has garnered the most international attention and acclaim, while at the same time arousing unexpected anger and protest. *Fire* is a film which explores a complex relationship between two sisters-in-law who find themselves in loveless, arranged marriages. Although having passed through the Indian censorship board unscathed, after three weeks the protests and demonstrations started.

*Earth* explores the tumultuous era when India and Pakistan were partitioned. *Water* (2005), was nominated for 5 Genie awards, for an Oscar and opened the world-renowned Toronto International Film Festival. The story about socially marginalized widows who are ostracized in conservative parts of India went through a series of delays as violent protesters destroyed her film set and threatened Deepa's life. Committed to the project, she eventually relocated the film shoot to Sri Lanka under a pseudonym.

Deepa also has a lighter side which was evidenced in the highly successful film *Bollywood, Hollywood* poking fun at traditional Indian stereotypes. Her latest film *Heaven on Earth* once again delves into thought provoking subject matter. The movie explores the life of a young Punjabi woman who finds herself in an abusive, arranged marriage with an Indo-Canadian man. The film debuted at the 2008 Toronto International Film Festival.

Deepa has been awarded numerous honors and recognition, and will continue to create films that provoke, cajole and enlighten.

Courtesy of Deepa Mehta

❧

*"Question everything around you and trust your inner instincts."*
—Deepa Mehta

❧

# Miriam Němcová

## Conductor, Czech Republic

When the lights go down and the conductor comes to the podium, most people will still expect to see a man. Why? Because in music, conducting is still heavily dominated by men. Yet, women like MIRIAM NĚMCOVÁ are breaking through the orchestra pit ceiling, demonstrating that not only can women be conductors, but that they can be exceptional.

Miriam began her conducting career at the age of sixteen with amateur choirs. She then pursued her studies in conducting and composition at the Prague Conservatory and the Prague Academy of Music. After graduating, Miriam began working with professional ensembles such as the Suk Chamber Orchestra, Karlovy Vary Symphony Orchestra, Hradec Kralove Philharmonic, the Czech Radio Choir and the Prague Philharmonic Choir.

She went to the Bach Academy in Stuttgart, Germany and later to the Conservatoire National Supérieur de Musique in Paris to pursue postgraduate studies. Upon her return she worked with opera companies in Prague and Liberec.

After her successful presentation of Verdi's Othello with the Ostrava Opera, Miriam was offered a position as chorus master and conductor with the Prague State Opera.

She has brought her unique brand of conducting to other countries around the world, such as when she presented Rossini's Barber of Seville in South Korea. Miriam also highlighted concert works of female composers in a performance with the New World Orchestra in Mexico City.

She continuously mentors up-and-coming performers in many countries, as well as through her role as Director of the Prague Conservatory's symphony orchestra, where she also teaches conducting.

In a profession where there are few female role models, young women are lucky to have someone like Miriam Němcová who has paved the path for other women to step up to the podium!

*"If a woman wants to make a living in a profession such as
conducting, which has traditionally been a male bastion,
she has to be better professionally prepared than any man.
Then she has to find a way which is consistent, but not offensive.
Till now this has worked for me!"*
—Miriam Němcová

# Della Reese

Singer, Actress, Entertainer, Author, Minister, USA

DELLA REESE is a name that is synonymous with entertainment par excellence. Trying to encapsulate her talents and career within a couple of pages is like trying to contain a tiger in a cardboard box. Although she may be most recognizable to many as the remarkable *Tess* in *Touched by an Angel*, she has had many parallel careers—singing, writing and producing music, acting, authoring books, and as a minister. Della has performed all with a brilliance that is transcendent. There are few people to whom the moniker "living legend" can be applied without exaggeration—Della Reese is one of these rare individuals.

She was born Deloreese Patricia Early in Detroit, Michigan in 1931 and she began singing in church when she was six years old. Throughout her formative years she was deeply involved in gospel singing and at 13, Della was hired by the late Mahalia Jackson to sing with her group. One of the lessons she learned from this association, which lasted three consecutive summers, was how to communicate with people through song, a lesson that Della has evolved into an art form.

While majoring in psychology at Wayne State University in Detroit, Della formed her own gospel group called "The Meditation Singers." However, due in part to the death of her mother, and her father's serious illness, Della had to interrupt her schooling to help support her family. The jobs she found ranged from clerical, to barbering, to truck driving and taxi driving.

The big break in her singing career came when the prize for a contest she won was a week singing at Detroit's famed *Flame Showbar*. She was so liked at this venue, that one week soon became eight.

While her roots were still in gospel music, Della was now being exposed to the talents and styles of such music greats as Ella Fitzgerald, Sarah Vaughn, Billie Holiday and others. In turn, Della developed an individual style that was her springboard to national prominence.

*"What has always worked for me—whatever I'm doing, thinking, feeling wondering—I put a little God in there."*
—Della Reese

# Della Reese, continued

She moved to New York City in 1953 and became a vocalist with the Erskine Hawkins Orchestra and soon signed her first recording contract. Her first recordings for Jubilee Records were *In the Still of the Night*, *I've Got My Love to Keep Me Warm*, and *Time after Time*.

In 1957, Della released a single called *And That Reminds Me*. After years of trying, Della finally had gained chart success with this song. It became a Top Twenty Pop hit for her that year and the record became a million-seller. In 1957, Billboard, Cashbox, and various other magazines voted Della as The Most Promising Singer.

In 1959, Della had moved on to another record company, RCA Records. She released her first single for RCA called *Don't You Know*, which was taken from Puccini's La Bohème. Acknowledgement from the music industry followed and she was nominated for a Grammy as best female vocalist. For the nine years that followed, Della performed regularly in Las Vegas, as well as touring across the U.S.

Della received a generous amount of television exposure following her recording successes. In the late 50's and 60's she appeared on many TV shows including *The Perry Como Show*, *The Jackie Gleason Show* and she had more than twenty appearances on the iconic *Ed Sullivan Show*.

She was the first female to be a guest host on the *The Tonight Show*, and in 1969 was asked to host a self-titled talk show making her the first black woman to host her own show.

Television saw a lot of Della over several decades, highlighting both her singing and comedic talents. She had appearances in such popular shows as *Sanford and Son*, *Night Court*, *Designing Women* and others. She became a regular cast member on *Chico and the Man* and then with Redd Foxx co-starred in the sit-com *The Royal Family*. Unfortunately, in both of these series the death of leading stars Freddie Prinz and Redd Foxx, respectively, resulted in their cancellation.

Della's action and dramatic side were evidenced when she guest starred in the *A-Team*, *L.A. Law*, *MacGyver* and *Nightmare in Badham County*, the latter which earned her an Emmy nomination.

Her most enduring and recognizable role was on the television series *Touched by an Angel*, which aired from 1994 through to 2003. Her character as the amazing "head" angel Tess has endeared her to many generations and for which she received three Emmy nominations, as well as Golden Globe and SAG nominations. Her television work has also been honored with a star on the Hollywood *Walk of Fame*.

Della has also been in several feature movies, including *Harlem Nights* with Eddie Murphy and Richard Pryor, and the more recent *Beauty Shop* also featuring Queen Latifah and Alicia Silverstone.

Enjoying what free time she has at home, Della now spends more time working on one of her other talents—writing. In fact her autobiography, *Angels Along the Way* was released to great reviews and *The God Inside of Me* became a best-selling children's book.

Besides being a singer and actress, Della is an ordained minister in the Understanding Principles for Better Living Church in Los Angeles, California, where every Sunday, she preaches her "Life Lessons" sermons to a capacity audience. This multi-racial, non-denominational church is known as the "UPChurch" reflecting her upbeat message and music.

Della has received many accolades and awards from numerous groups including having Oprah Winfrey honor Della at her Legends Ball ceremony along with 25 other African-American women. The National Association for the Advancement of Colored People (NAACP) Image Awards, which celebrates the outstanding achievements and performances of people of color in the arts as well as those individuals or groups who promote social justice, has recognized Della seven times, a testament to the positive influence she has in the community.

Della has not given up her first love, singing. She still performs in concert halls, nightclubs and music festivals. More and more she is being asked to perform with symphony orchestras, receiving unanimous acclaim from critics and audiences alike.

Her favorite venues in which to perform are festivals/fairs and nightclubs. As Della says, "the intimacy between me and a nightclub audience is unmatched, for we become as one, while on the other hand, the combination of being outdoors and the surging crowds of a festival, creates such an excitement in me that it makes me want to give more and more of myself."

The world is lucky that she continues to give more of herself, because her fans have never been able to get enough of Della Reese!

# Pamela D. Wallin

## Journalist, TV Host, Diplomat, Entrepreneur, Author, Canada

PAMELA WALLIN's career is the result of saying "yes." She has never turned down an interesting job offer, even if she initially thought that she knew little about the role. The reality is that she knew more than she thought which gave way to many successful career directions.

Pamela credits much of her success to the lessons learned growing up in a small town in one of Canada's prairie provinces. Her parents imbued her with a sense of confidence, an eagerness to excel and a heightened sense of integrity.

After graduating from university with a degree in psychology and political science, she began working as a prison social worker. Her career in the media was set in motion by chance, when a friend called needing a one-week replacement for an open-line radio host and she jumped at the opportunity.

Pamela continued to pursue a career in journalism and in 1985 became the first woman in Canadian television history to become a bureau chief, and then in 1992 became the first woman in Canada to co-host the nightly national newscast. Unfortunately for Pamela, the constant re-tooling of the program by the broadcaster led to poor ratings and much to the surprise of Pamela and the rest of Canada, it was cancelled.

Undaunted, in 1995 she founded her own independent television company through which she hosted and produced a live nightly interview program. As well, she hosted the Canadian edition of *Who Wants to be a Millionaire*, which at the time, garnered the highest ratings ever for a network production in that country.

When the Prime Minister of Canada called and offered her the position of Consul General of Canada in New York, she accepted even though she didn't quite know what a Consul General did. Yet with her customary enthusiasm, she embraced the opportunity and excelled in the role.

In 2001, Pamela spoke publicly about her very personal battle with colorectal cancer, a battle she fought and won.

Currently she is the Senior Advisor on Canada-US Relations to the President of the Americas Society and the Council of the Americas, as well as the Chancellor of the University of Guelph. She sits on several corporate boards and is affiliated with numerous charitable organizations.

She has been awarded 14 honorary doctorates, is an Officer of the Order of Canada, a member of the Broadcasting Hall of Fame, and has been twice honored by Queen Elizabeth II for her public service and achievements. In her "spare" time, she has authored three books.

Pamela has always been generous with her time in assisting worthwhile causes and individuals, as she is determined to positively change the world.

Courtesy of Pamela D. Wallin

*"My parents taught me through deed, not just word, perhaps the single most important of life's lessons—and it's my shorthand, not their's—but the message was clear:*

**Character Trumps Genius**

*Simply put, you can be smart, but if you are not kind and decent, fair and generous—when it is difficult to do so—then all the brains in the world are for naught...."*
—Pamela D. Wallin

Sandra Faber
*USA*

Patty Wagstaff
*USA*

Mae Jemison
*USA*

# Reach for the Stars

At night, when the sky is bright we look up and we wonder what it would be like to transcend into the heavens and be at one with the universe. In this segment you will find three women who have "touched" the stars in their own unique ways.

The astronomer provides meaning through providing scientific research and explanation; the astronaut has seen the earth from the vantage point of a space shuttle and is someone who has literally touched the stars; and finally the aerobatic pilot who thrills with her ability to defy gravity in her flying machine. Each of these women has not only sought, but also grasped, their own piece of the cosmos.

# Sandra Faber

## Professor, Researcher—Astronomy, Astrophysics, USA

While most of us are out at night, looking to the heavens and "wishing upon a star," Dr. SANDRA FABER is working on taking the mystery out of the night skies through research focused on the formation and evolution of galaxies and the universe. She is a University Professor of Astronomy and Astrophysics at the University of California, Santa Cruz and performs research at California's Lick Observatory.

As a child, Sandra always loved science, so much so that as a teenager her favorite pastime was learning math, science and doing homework and of course, reading the science fiction of Andre Norton, Ray Bradbury and Isaac Asimov. Although she enjoyed spending the evenings with her father looking at the night sky, it wasn't until she started at Swarthmore College that she came to study astronomy.

She wasn't sure about the mechanism of science or how you could be a scientist. Sandra didn't know that people could actually make money being a college professor and doing research. There weren't any women role models to look up to.

At Swarthmore, Sandra initially pursued two branches of science—astronomy and chemistry. But she didn't find chemistry fundamental enough for her. Physics was more in line with her way of thinking and at Swarthmore physics was a requirement to become an astronomer.

She went on to Harvard University for two years of graduate studies, and then followed her husband to Washington DC, where she worked independently on her PhD thesis, discovering a correlation between the size of a galaxy and the strength of the absorption lines in its spectrum.

Her pioneering research led to several monumental discoveries such as the Faber-Jackson relation, which provides a method for determining the distances to galaxies. Sandra is currently working on research, the aim of which is to disentangle the age of stars in elliptical galaxies, with the result apparently being that many of these stellar populations are found to be surprisingly young. Sandra is also conducting several projects on the Hubble Space Telescope. She currently does most of her work with graduate students and has several ongoing collaborations with former students, which have lasted many years.

Sandra has won numerous awards over the years including Best American Scientists under 40 in 1984, NASA Group Achievement Award, 1993, and Discover Magazine's 50 Best American Women Scientists in 2003.

When Sandra looks out into the night sky she sees a vast mystery which is just waiting to be unveiled—her version of "wishing upon a star."

Courtesy of Dr. Sandra Faber

*"My advice is very simple: pick a small number of things and do them well. Be ruthless, throw out all unnecessary things. You can do one thing well, probably two, but maybe not three and certainly not four. Examples of 'things': scientific researcher, spouse, mother, community worker, teacher, public speaker, fundraiser, popular writer. Choose, focus and go for it!"*
—Dr. Sandra Faber

67

# Mae Jemison

## Astronaut, Entrepreneur, Physician, Engineer, Dancer, USA

When Dr. MAE JEMISON was a young girl growing up on the south side of Chicago, she watched the telecasts of the Gemini and Apollo space flights and knew this was her destiny. It didn't matter that all the astronauts of the time were white and male; she knew that one day she too would be a space traveler. In September 1992, she achieved that goal on the space shuttle Endeavour—the first woman of color to do so.

Mae is the quintessential Renaissance woman. Besides her six year stretch as an astronaut at NASA, she is also a physician, chemical engineer, educator, jazz dancer and choreographer. She defies categorization and is convinced that the only true limits are the ones that we impose on ourselves or permit others to impose on us.

Mae's parents stressed education and exploration. They let her spend many hours in the libraries reading about astronomy and the other sciences and encouraged her affection for science novels and space flight. Growing up, one of Mae's favorite TV shows was *Star Trek*, a fictional program about space exploration, where she found inspiration through the character of Lieutenant Uhura, played by the African American actress, Nichelle Nichols. In 1993 Mae actually appeared on an episode of *Star Trek: The Next Generation* becoming the only real astronaut ever to appear on any of the Star Trek series.

Mae Jemison entered Stanford University at the young age of 16 on a scholarship, majoring in chemical engineering and African and Afro-American studies. She graduated in 1977.

Mae always had a great love for dancing, which she started at the age of 9. In her senior year of college, she was trying to decide whether to become a professional dancer or to pursue another love of hers—medicine—and become a doctor. Her mother told her that she could always dance if she was a doctor, but she couldn't doctor if she was a dancer. Mae headed for Cornell University where she earned her medical degree.

Her wanderlust and desire to help the disadvantaged of the world resulted in her spending two and a half years with the Peace Corps as a Medical Officer for Sierra Leone and Liberia in West Africa. Throughout her career, her work has taken her to countries across the world including working in a Cambodian refugee camp and with the Flying Doctors of East Africa.

Mae entered private medical practice in Los Angeles in 1985 and at the same time began attending graduate engineering courses. It was around this time that she applied to NASA for the astronaut program and was accepted in 1987—one of 15 candidates from over 2000 applications. Finally she rocketed for the stars on September 12, 1992 where she served as the first Science Mission Specialist performing experiments in material science, life science and human adaption to weightlessness.

Mae resigned from NASA in 1993, and founded the Jemison Group, a technology consulting firm which considered the socio-economical impacts when designing technologies. In 1999 she founded BioSentient Corporation, a company focused on improving health and human performance.

Mae founded an international youth science camp, chairs the Dorothy Jemison Foundation for Excellence and serves as Bayer Corporation's national advocate for the *Making Science Make Sense* initiative. She has been recognized for her achievements receiving honorary doctorates from leading universities and being inducted into several Halls of Fame. In 1993 Mae was hailed as one of People Magazine's "World's 50 Most Beautiful People."

If that little girl growing up in Chicago could see Mae today, she would be smiling. As Mae once said, "the best way to make your dreams come true is to wake up." It looks like Dr. Mae Jemison has been awake all her life!

Courtesy of Mae Jemison

*"One of the most important pieces of advice I can give to women I wrote in my book "Find Where the Wind Goes," and the advice is this: Pay attention to learn from all the adventures you've had in life, big and small, for within each, there is valuable insight to help you throughout life. The lessons that happen when satisfying our curiosity, but which appear to conflict with maintaining our dignity, are particularly important."*
—Dr. Mae Jemison

# Patty Wagstaff

## Champion Aerobatic Pilot, USA

If you've ever visited the Smithsonian National Air and Space Museum in Washington, D.C. you would have seen PATTY WAGSTAFF"s Goodrich Extra 260 airplane in the Pioneers of Flight Gallery. It's right next to Amelia Earhart's Lockheed Vega, a true testament to Patty's trailblazer status in the world of aviation.

To Patty Wagstaff the sky represents adventure, freedom and challenge. A six-time member of the US Aerobatic Team, Patty has won the gold, silver and bronze medals in Olympic-level international aerobatic competition. She was the first woman to win the title of US National Aerobatic champion, one of the few people to win it three times. She is particularly proud of receiving the airshow industry's most prestigious award, the "Sword of Excellence," and the "Bill Barber Award for Showmanship." Patty is also a six-time recipient of the "First Lady of Aerobatics" Betty Skelton Award. She has been inducted into the National Aviation Hall of Fame.

Born in the USA, Patty grew up in and around airplanes. The family moved to Japan when she was nine years old where her father was a Captain for Japan Air Lines. At ten years old, when her father let her take the controls of his aircraft, her lifelong love affair with airplanes began.

Patty's first experience with bush flying was not a positive one—the airplane she chartered crashed on its first flight. So Patty learned to fly herself. She then went on to earn her Commercial, Instrument, Seaplane and Commercial Helicopter Ratings. Patty is a Flight and Instrument Instructor and is rated and qualified to fly many airplanes, from World War II warbirds to jets. Patty's sister, Toni, is also a pilot and a Captain for Continental Airlines.

Though she had never seen aerobatics, a lifelong curiosity led her to attend her first airshow in Abbotsford, British Columbia in 1983, where she saw aerobatic pilots perform and promised herself "I can do that!" By 1985, five years after gaining her pilot's license, she earned a spot on the US Aerobatic Team.

Patty has trained with the Russian Aerobatic Team and has flown in airshows and competitions in such exotic places as South America, Russia, Europe, Mexico and Iceland. She is a member of the Screen Actors Guild, Motion Picture Pilots Association, United Stuntwomen's Association, working as a stunt pilot and aerial coordinator for the film and television industry.

Continuing a life of experience and adventure, Patty's other interests include her Jack Russell Terriers, her parrots and riding her horse training for show jumping competitions.

She is a stunning example of how finding meaningful expression for your innate personality and talents can truly change your life.

*"People talk a lot about 'passion' and while 'passion' is an important component of leading a full life, I think it's an overused and under explained word. For me it means that a person should follow the path that makes them happy. People might tell you to follow another path— go to a certain school or college; take a certain job, etc.—and it might be easier to do what you are told, what has been prescribed for you, but if you are not happy or don't feel right about going in that direction then you'll never find what 'passion' really means.*

*Passion means that you, before anyone else, have to be happy with your choices. If you are not happy in your life then you will not be able to make anyone else happy— your children, your husband, your friends.*

*So the one piece of advice I would give is to follow the path that makes you happiest, that feels right. Trust your intuition to guide you and dig deep into your soul and listen to yourself and what your heart tells you, and have faith that the future is inside of you. Then you can create the energy to make whatever it is you want happen."*
—Patty Wagstaff

Kim Baird
*Canada*

Joanne
Hayes-White
*USA*

Angela
Salinas
*USA*

Hazel McCallion
*Canada*

Claudia J.
Kennedy
*USA*

Dame Calliopa
Pearlette Louisy
*St, Lucia*

Erin Pizzey
*England*

Yolanda
Kakabadse Navarro
*Ecuador*

# To Serve and Protect

Neelie Kroes
*Belgium*

Olga Abramova
*Belarus*

Claudia Fritsche
*Liechtenstein*

Sima Samar
*Afghanistan*

Lady Justice
Joyce Aluoch
*Kenya*

"To serve and protect" is a term that is often used as a mission statement by police forces and the like. In *1 Piece of Advice* the term is given a much broader mandate. There are many ways that the following women serve—with their commitment to public service—and protect—our security, our human rights, our First Nations and our environment.

These are stories of women who have committed themselves, sometimes at great personal sacrifice, to create a society that is just and fair in all four corners of the globe. They are often the voice for those people or causes that others have chosen to ignore. Yet with these women at the helm, with their proud voices and commitment, everyone has been, is and will be, given a strong voice.

Dame
Catherine Tizard
*New Zealand*

# Olga Abramova

## Former Deputy of the Belarussian Government

OLGA ABRAMOVA has always remained faithful to the electoral slogan which she used many years ago—"One Land. One Nation. One Life to Succeed in Assisting People." It is this slogan which has defined Olga Abramova's actions throughout her life.

She was born in 1953 in Minsk, the capital of Belarus. Always a good student she dreamed first of becoming a geologist and later an artist. But inevitably she went on to the Belarussian State University where she decided to study sociology and philosophy. She taught these subjects in university for 20 years, along the way earning her PhD. As one of the most renowned political scientists in Belarus, several of Olga's works have been published in Belarussian, Russian and German journals.

Eventually she turned her attention to politics as a way of effecting positive change in her country. Olga chose to join the political party "Yabloko" which she believed would help to create within Belarus a European style social democratic system of government. She has been the leader of Yabloko in Belarus since 1997.

In 2004 she was elected the Deputy of the Belarussian parliament for the third time. She has always been an independent thinker and when the Belarussian parliament passed a Bill in 2007 which was to put an end to social benefits for hundreds of thousands of students, disabled and retired people, Olga was the lone dissenting voice voting against it. Why? Because Olga felt that the Bill and its ramifications should have been made public so that those affected could provide input prior to its finalization.

In September 2008, Olga was not re-elected to the parliament of Belarus, in an election, the authenticity of which has been questioned. The

---

* Press Release: September 29, 2008, Organization for Security and Cooperation in Europe: Minsk, Belarus

Organization for Security and Co-operation in Europe (OSCE) which was monitoring the election stated in a press release:

"The count was assessed as bad or very bad in 48 per cent of polling stations visited. Where access was possible, several cases of deliberate falsification of results were observed."*

Olga Abramova's life is her slogan and we know that she will continue to work to do the right thing—a living testament to her belief "…One Life to Succeed in Assisting People."

*"Learn to say 'NO!' "*
—Olga Abramova

# Lady Justice Joyce Aluoch

## Judge, Court of Appeal, Kenya

JOYCE ALUOCH's late father decided she should become a lawyer. One day he put Joyce into his car and drove her to the Kenya School of Law to introduce her to the Principal. Shortly after that, she was called for an interview and so began her remarkable career in law. Today Lady Justice Joyce Aluoch is one of 16 female judges in Kenya, the only woman judge on the nine Judge Kenyan Court of Appeal and the senior most woman judge serving in Kenya's judiciary today.

Joyce grew up in a busy household, where there were six girls and four boys. Her father was a District Commissioner in pre-independent Kenya and her mother ran the household. She credits her father as being a major influence in her life. She remembers admiring not only the administrative position he held, but also the way he dressed. "He wore smart starched khaki shorts, a starched khaki jacket and a cap on his head. That is how he left the house going to work everyday and I just thought this was so smart and special."

She entered the judiciary straight out of Law School, when she became a District Magistrate for the Juvenile Court. Several other appointments, all of increasing responsibility, followed—Resident Magistrate, Senior Resident Magistrate and then the Head of the Family Division High Court, and finally as Judge on the Court of Appeal. Throughout her distinguished career she has served on many national and international committees, associations and task forces focused on helping women and children. These included the United Nations Committee on the Rights of the Child, the International Tribunal for Children's Rights (Canada, Great Britain, and Bosnia/Herzegovina), the Task Force on the Implementation of the new Sexual Offences Act in Kenya, and a patron of the Kenya Women Judges Association. Working with other volunteers, she designed the 2002 Peer Prevention Education Program on HIV/AIDS for Girls and Young Women, which was voted best overall program at the 2002 World's AIDS conference and today is a model being used in many countries.

Yet Joyce's journey was not without its speed bumps. She encountered obstacles in her ascent which were related to her being a woman in a male dominated occupation. It took too long for her to get her promotion to the Court of Appeal, even though she was qualified. However as Joyce says, "I kept working hard, never gave up, and at God's own timing, I got my promotion. No woman who believes she is qualified for a position should ever give up."

Joyce Aluoch never gives up. She continues to augment her knowledge having just completed a Global Master of Arts program at the Fletcher School of Law and Diplomacy at Tufts University in Boston. The President of Kenya acknowledged her many achievements when she received the Elder of the Burning Spear Award, which recognized her for human rights and humanitarian work.

It is obvious that Joyce has passed on her approach and attitude to her three daughters, Brenda, Sandra and Connie, who are an investments banker/commercial lawyer, an IT specialist and a Fashion Designer, respectively. Yet most assuredly Joyce has succeeded in inspiring many young women in Kenya, to aim high and to strive to be the best.

*"My secret in life has been first, to believe in myself, my ability to perform. Secondly and with God's help, I have moved forward to accomplish my goals. This has not been easy and there have been many hurdles on the way, but the fact that I have come this far is testimony that it can be done and in fact, it has been done. Women must strive to achieve their set goals. It comes from within oneself—it is never given on a silver platter"*
—Judge Joyce Aluoch

# Kim Baird

## Chief of the Tsawwassen First Nation, Canada

In 1999, at the age of twenty-nine, KIM BAIRD became the youngest woman to be elected as Chief of the Tsawwassen First Nation in the Canadian province of British Columbia (B.C.). She made history by negotiating B.C.'s first land treaty for her community, estimated to be worth $120 million. She prides herself on giving the Tsawwassen First Nations people a sense of control over their destiny. Clearly they agree with her vision, having re-elected her four times.

Kim's path to leadership was not without its trials. At the age of fourteen, when Kim went to live on the reserve of the Tsawwassen First Nation, she was shocked by the conditions of isolation, poverty and the sense of hopelessness she witnessed. As a typical teenager of her time, growing up in a suburb of Vancouver, one of Canada's largest and most beautiful cities, she had been sheltered from the harsh conditions the people on the reserve faced. Suddenly it was she who was the target of prejudice and discrimination, with former friends being forbidden to associate with her. Nevertheless, she persevered and became the first in her community to graduate from high school in over twenty years.

During her years in college Kim learned about the history of the poor relations between aboriginal peoples and the ruling governments. The status and rights of women of the First Nations communities lagged behind those of the rest of Canadian women. The Indian Act, introduced in 1876, ensured that politically, men had all the power. The act prohibited women the right to vote, hold office or even to speak at public meetings. Women were not allowed to become chiefs until the act was changed in 1951. In fact, First Nations' women did not have the right to vote in Canadian elections prior to the 1960's! Remarkably, when most would have focused on the stark realities, Kim looked beyond. In her own words, she "became inspired" to bring about positive change.

Foregoing the usual activities of her age group, Kim entered the political arena while still in her late teens. At age 20, she founded a research department for aboriginal land claims. At 23, Kim became a member of the band council and at 26, she took a negotiating course at Harvard University. All of this laid the ground work for her election to the position of Chief in 1999.

Chief Baird is remarkably skilled at multitasking. In addition to being Chief, she sits on the BC Hydro Board of Directors, the First Nations Employment Society's Board of Directors, the Vancouver Aboriginal Skills and Employment Program the Naut'samawt Tribal Council and the Joe Mathias Scholarship Foundation. Kim is also a devoted mother of two very young daughters and is working towards her Bachelor of Arts degree at the University of British Columbia.

Chief Kim Baird is absolutely determined to heal her community through employment and self-determination, thereby ensuring a better future for following generations. She has given her community and all those who know her, the gift of hope.

Courtesy of Chief Kim Baird

*"When in a leadership role—be yourself! You don't need to change your style to emulate somebody else. Your own style is the most effective way to promote change within your own personal life and career."*
—Chief Kim Baird

# Claudia Fritsche

## Ambassador of the Principality of Liechtenstein to the United States of America

CLAUDIA FRITSCHE had a long way to go before she became her country's first Ambassador to the United Nations. When she was growing up in Liechtenstein, girls did not have access to secondary education unless their parents could afford to send them to boarding school abroad.

After leaving the "Higher Education for Daughters Institute of St. Elisabeth," a business secretarial school run by Catholic nuns, Claudia worked for one year as a secretary in a law firm. It was at this time that she became the personal assistant to the newly elected prime minister of Liechtenstein. Although her political consciousness did not yet exist, it quickly developed.

When her party lost the election and a new prime minister was elected, Claudia decided to travel the world with her then husband-to-be. They traveled throughout Australia and South Africa, financing their trips through odd jobs. Four years later her party won the government majority again and she was recruited back to government service with the offer to help establish the Office of Foreign Affairs which until then had been part of the Prime Minister's Office. She agreed to return under the condition that she would eventually be trained as a diplomat, a term they readily accepted despite the fact that she had no university education.

Claudia subsequently worked within the Office of Foreign Affairs. She represented her country at a number of international conferences and assumed positions within the Liechtenstein Embassy in Switzerland and Austria, including serving as First Secretary and Chargée d'Affaires. As Permanent Representative of Liechtenstein to the Council of Europe in Strasbourg, Claudia represented the Liechtenstein Government on the European committee on Equality between Women and Men.

While preparing her country's admission into the United Nations, Claudia applied for a job which did not yet exist. She was determined to represent

Liechtenstein at the United Nations in New York. H.S.H. Prince Hans-Adam von Liechtenstein appointed her Ambassador to the UN in August 1990.

Claudia moved to New York and served in this capacity until 2002 when she was asked to establish yet another new diplomatic representation for Liechtenstein, namely the Embassy in Washington, D.C.

Claudia Fritsche still serves as the Ambassador of the Principality of Liechtenstein to the United States, a testimony to what can be accomplished if one focuses on the possibilities, even when no one else yet knew they existed!

Courtesy of Claudia Fritsche

*"PLAN—your life. Equip yourself with the best possible education. You may or may not meet 'Mr. Right.' You may or may not have a family. One day you may be alone and may be responsible for more people than yourself— i.e., your children, your parents.*

*TRUST—your instincts, your gut feeling. You know when something feels right and when it does not.*

*BELIEVE—in love, in dreams, in wonders, in magic but first and foremost, believe in yourself.*

*LISTEN—out of respect for others and because you can always learn something.*

*HAVE A LIFE—nurture friendships, start a hobby, read (books), write (by hand)."*

—Claudia Fritsche

# Joanne Hayes-White

## Chief, San Francisco Fire Department, USA

When someone yells "FIRE!" most people will instinctively run away. Well, JOANNE HAYES-WHITE chose a career where she is running into a building on fire, while others are running out. She is the first female Chief of the San Francisco Fire Department (SFFD), which is the largest urban fire department in the world to have a woman at the helm. She began serving as Chief in 2004.

Joanne never envisioned the fire service as a viable career option even though she loved red fire engines. This was partially as a result that while growing up there was no role model that looked like her. In fact, until 1987, the SFFD was an all-male workforce with all the personnel referred to as "firemen."

Joanne graduated from the University of Santa Clara with a degree in business that she used in her role as Human Resource Administrator for a hospital in San Francisco. Yet the "siren song" of the fire department soon caught her attention and in 1990 she joined the SFFD, which only 9 women had done before her. This is a testament to Joanne, thriving on challenge. "If someone says you can't do that, I'm going to try my hardest and prove I can do it."

Being one of the first few females in the department wasn't always easy for Joanne, but she had city roots and a lot of commonalities with some of the firefighters which helped her along the way. She also had numerous mentors who responded enthusiastically to her obvious quest for knowledge and understanding.

Over her almost two decade career with the department she is proud that she has worked either as a firefighter or officer at every one of San Francisco's forty-two fire stations and that she knows many of the 1800 firefighters by name (15% of whom today are women).

Her ascent to Chief didn't happen overnight. After being a firefighter for 3 years, she was promoted to Lieutenant, then Captain, Battalion Chief and then Assistant Deputy Chief in 1998. Prior to her appointment as Chief, she served as the Director of Training for the SFFD.

Joanne was having dinner with her family, when she received a page from the Mayor's office with the indication that he would be asking her to be Chief the next day. This was only a few days after she was told the Mayor was considering her for the role, which the mother of three young boys was not even pursuing.

She has been recognized several times as one of San Francisco's Most Influential Women, as well as being hailed as one of the Top 100 Irish Americans. Joanne is a firm believer in community involvement and the department's participation in the community has noticeably increased during her tenure. Joanne, herself, serves on the Boards of the American Red Cross (Bay Area Chapter), the Hibernian Newman Club, and Mercy High School—the high school where she attended and was senior class president.

She lives and breathes the teamwork ethos everyday, and would never ask someone to do something she isn't willing to do or can't do herself. In firefighting, teamwork can mean the difference between life and death.

For Joanne, becoming the Chief of the SFFD is a dream come true. She is "humbled by being in this position, and as she says, "I wouldn't be here without such a supportive network of family and friends."

*"Timing may not always be the best, however when opportunity knocks, open the door with confidence and walk straight through!"*
—Chief Joanne Hayes-White

# Yolanda Kakabadse Navarro

## Environmentalist, Ecuador

Long before it was fashionable, YOLANDA KAKABADSE NAVARRO was committed to the environment. She has noted that ensuring the viability of the environment is as simple as the logic of survival—if you live in harmony with nature you will survive, and if you don't there is no option for life.

Yolanda was born and has lived her entire life in Ecuador, a country known for its biodiversity and includes the environmentally rich Galapagos Islands. It is no wonder that the young Yolanda, marvelling at the vast expanses of nature in her country, came to be passionate about ensuring its continued existence.

She has been an environmental leader since 1979 when she co-founded Fundación Natura in Ecuador, to this day one of the world's most effective national environmental non-government organizations. She went on to become Ecuador's Minister of the Environment, then served two terms as President of the International Union for the Conservation of Nature, the world's largest association of conservation agencies and organizations, until 2004.

More recently she founded the Foundation for the Future of Latin America ("FFLA") and acts as the organization's Senior Advisor. FFLA has been a leader in conflict resolution around environmental issues in Latin America.

Yolanda is a strong moral leader, who has written and often spoken on the role of ethics in globalization. She is a member of the Board of Directors of the Ford Foundation and the Inter-American dialogue which is the leading U.S. center for policy analysis, exchange, and communication on issues in Western Hemisphere affairs. She is a member of the Environmental Advisory Board at Coca-Cola, was recently inducted as the first member of the Wildlife Trust Alliance Advisory Council, and previously served on the Board of the World Wide Fund for Nature—International, among others.

Yolanda has had many honors bestowed upon her including Global 500 Award of the United Nations Environment Programme, the Golden Ark Order bestowed by Prince Bernard of the Netherlands, and the Zayed Prize in 2001, the world's highest environmental prize.

She has said that her passion for the environment could qualify as a virus—once you get it, you cannot get rid of it. Here's hoping that Yolanda never finds a cure for her particular "environmental passion virus!"

Courtesy of Yolanda Kakabadse Navarro

*"There is always something good in the problems*
*and obstacles you face. Look for it!"*
—Yolanda Kakabadse Navarro

# Claudia J. Kennedy

## Lieutenant General US Army (Retired), USA

Surprisingly, it was not the fact that her father was a career soldier that resulted in CLAUDIA KENNEDY deciding on a career in the U.S. Army. It was a chance encounter with an ad in Cosmopolitan magazine in the late 60's.

According to Claudia, the postman found a copy of Cosmopolitan without a mailing label in his bag, and knowing a college girl was living at her address, put it in the box. As she was reading about all the hot fashions and dating advice, she spotted a full-page ad with the caption "Be an Intelligence Analyst" with applicants being sought for the Women's Army Corps. And the rest, as they say, is history.

Growing up in the 50's and 60's, Claudia initially thought that the only professions open to women were either teaching or nursing, but her father suggested she consider being a doctor. Quickly coming to the realization that medicine was not for her, she eventually went to Southwestern University in Memphis to pursue a degree in Philosophy. As she progressed through university, Claudia began to wonder what kind of job she would get to fill the years between graduation and the inevitability of marriage and motherhood. And that is when the Cosmopolitan showed up.*

What originally was intended to be a two year commitment, resulted in a 31 year distinguished career where Claudia Kennedy became the first woman to achieve the rank of three-star general in the United States Army, in the position of Deputy Chief of Staff for Army Intelligence (1997-2000). She oversaw policies and operations affecting 45,000 people stationed world wide with a budget of nearly $1 billion.

During her career she commanded a company, an intelligence battalion, a recruiting battalion and an intelligence brigade. As a general officer, she served as the senior intelligence officer for the U.S. Forces Command, Deputy Commanding General for the Army Intelligence Center and School, completing her career as the Deputy Chief of Staff for Intelligence.

She has been a vociferous advocate for women in uniform to report incidents of harassment, after she brought harassment charges against an equal

*"Tell the truth. Tell the absolute truth. Sometimes it is hard to be both truthful and kind. But it is always possible to find a way to be both.*

*Make sure someone else knows what you know. As a lawyer in the Pentagon told me when I first arrived: 'Do not have secrets.'*

*Even when I have thought the truth was difficult or did not reflect well on me, it always proved to have been a wise choice to have told the truth and to have had no secrets."*

—Claudia J. Kennedy

rank general in the late 90's. "If discrimination or misconduct is not reported at an appropriate time, then public policy may never change."**

General Kennedy has received numerous honors and awards during her military career, including the National Intelligence Distinguished Service Medal, the Army Distinguished Service Medal and four Legions of Merits which are awarded for "exceptionally meritorious conduct in the performance of outstanding services and achievements."

She has been named to a list of "Best Women Role Models," and Vanity Fair's "Most Influential" list. She was also named to the Ladies Home Journal's list of "100 Most Important Women." General Kennedy has been honored for leadership and lifetime achievement by many organizations. Other organizations which have honored her achievements including the Business and Professional Women (USA), Women Executives and State Government, National Women's Law Center, the National Center for Women and Policy, and the Volunteers of America.

Since completing her Army career, Claudia Kennedy has lived in Fairfax County, Virginia, and Hilton Head Island, South Carolina. The memoir of her life and time in the military, *Generally Speaking*, was published in September 2001. She is on the Employment Practices Advisory Panel of Wal-Mart and is on the boards of Essex Corporation, VT Griffin, Opportunity International, The White House Project, Population Action International, The Third Way, SecureUS, and Intelligent Decisions, Inc. She has appeared as a military consultant for NBC and CNN, and recently gave a keynote address at the Democratic National Convention in support of Barack Obama, who inevitably went on to win the US Presidential election.

* Reference: *Generally Speaking* by Claudia Kennedy—Grand Central Publishing—2001
** New York Times: May 13, 2000, *General Urges Women to Tell of Harassment*

# Neelie Kroes

## European Commissioner for Competition, Belgium

NEELIE KROES is the current European Commissioner for Competition and has been a staple of the Forbes 100 list of Most Powerful Women in the World for several years.

When she was appointed to this role in 2004—the first woman to hold this post—she was not the "frontrunner." Initially her nomination was heavily criticized because of her perceived ties to big business—the very enterprises which her role would require her to police. Over the years, Neelie won over her previous critics and has proven both her integrity and business acumen. Her directness and straight talking approach as a tough defender of free markets has earned her the nickname "Nickel Neelie."

She has had an impressive career in both business and politics. After receiving her Masters of Science in Economics in 1965, she spent part of her career in the family transport business and as a professor at the Erasmus University. It was however, in 1971 when she began her ascent in politics, first as a member of parliament in the Netherlands. She served as the Dutch State Secretary of Transport and Water Management from 1977 to 1981 and subsequently was appointed as the Minister of the same department. She was responsible for the privitization of both the postal and telephone services in the Netherlands.

After leaving her post as minister, Neelie served on the boards of various Dutch companies and from 1991 to 2000 was the Chairwoman of Nyenrode University, a prestigious private Dutch business school. Until her appointment as European Commissioner in 2004, she was an advisor and board member of several national and international companies.

In 2008 Neelie was awarded the prestigious Kiel Institute Global Economy Prize, the first woman to receive this honor, which is given in recognition of ground-breaking thinking and mediation in the challenging times of globalization. Her contributions have also been recognized by other awards including being named Knight of the Order of the Dutch Lion, and Grand Officer of the Orange–Nassau of the Netherlands. In 2008 she was named as one of Time Magazine's 100 Most Influential People.

Neelie is a passionate advocate for greater representation of women in senior business and political positions and considers her function as a role model and mentor of women as a great privilege.

Courtesy © European Community

*"NEVER GIVE UP!"*
*—Neelie Kroes*

# Dame Calliopa Pearlette Louisy

## Governor General, St. Lucia

Her Excellency Dame CALLIOPA PEARLETTE LOUISY is the first woman to hold the office of Governor-General of Saint Lucia. She was born on June 8, 1946 in the southern village of Laborie, St. Lucia, where she received most of her early education.

She obtained a Bachelor's degree, from the University of West Indies, in English and French after having been awarded a scholarship through the Canadian International Development Agency. She then went on to earn another scholarship to obtain a Masters Degree in Linguistics from Laval University in Quebec, after which she went to the University of Bristol in England to earn a PhD in Education.

Throughout Dame Louisy's entire professional life, she has pursued her passion for education in her roles as a teacher, principal and dean, in various educational institutions. To this day she continues her research into education and small state issues, with her articles being published in international journals and publications.

She has been bestowed with numerous awards including:

- International Woman of the Year by the International Biographical Center (1998 and 2001)
- Dame Grand Cross of the Most Distinguished Order of St. Michael and St. George by Queen Elizabeth II (1999)
- Dame of Grace of the Most Venerable Order of St. John (2001)
- Dame of The Equestrian Order of St. Gregory the Great, a Papal award (2002)
- Inducted as a Paul Harris Fellow, Rotary International (2001)
- Caribbean Luminary Award by the American Foundation of the University of the West Indies (2007)

Dame Louisy's recognition speaks to the amazing woman she is. When emailing her a thank you for her contribution to this book, she wrote back, within a short period of time stating:

*"I hope my small contribution can be of help to someone. That's the principle I've learned to live by, and it has helped me cope with quite a few challenges in my day."*

She is truly someone who ensures that she makes her life about contributing positively each and every moment!

*"In life, one needs to learn to look beyond the constraints of the moment and dedicate one's energies to doing one's best during trying times. This is how one can position oneself, little by little to take advantage of the opportunities of the future when these present themselves."*
—Dame Calliopa Pearlette Louisy

# Hazel McCallion

## Mayor, Canada

Mayor HAZEL MCCALLION is often affectionately referred to as "Hurricane Hazel" for her vibrant and outspoken style of no-nonsense politics. In 2006 she was elected for the eleventh consecutive term to head the City of Mississauga, Canada's sixth largest city, garnering 91% of the votes.

Hazel began her mayoral career at 56, an age when many others are thinking of retirement. But for this dynamo, thirty years after first taking office, retirement has never been a consideration.

She was born in Quebec in 1921, where her father owned a fishing and canning company, and her mother, a homemaker, ran the family farm. After high school, she wanted to attend university but financially, the family could not afford it. So she attended business secretarial school and then began working in Montreal. It was after she transferred to Toronto that she met and married Sam McCallion.

While raising three children, Hazel and her husband founded "The Mississauga Booster," a community based newspaper. Hazel was always interested in improving her community and by the time she was elected mayor, she had sat on virtually every committee in her region and also served on the executive of many provincial and federal committees and associations.

Hazel is well known for her love of hockey, a game which, to this day, she still plays recreationally (she played for a professional women's team while attending school in Montreal).

She has overseen the growth of Mississauga from a small collection of towns and villages to one of Canada's largest cities. Her approach and attitude have resulted in many awards and recognitions, including ranking as number 2 in the World Mayor's poll in 2005.

She has received the Order of Canada, has had several academic buildings named after her, and has been named one of the "American Women of the Year" in 2001 in the Who's Who of American Women. US television talk show host Regis Philbin was recently in Mississauga to help Hazel celebrate her 30th year as Mayor.

And, of course, no profile of Hazel's would be complete without mentioning the bobble-head dolls which were made in her likeness!

Courtesy of the City of Mississauga

*"I consider it a blessing to have a job that I love. Having a life filled with meaning and purpose and living my life in a Christian-like manner helps to motivate me and keep me energized.*

*In this vein, my advice to women would be to strive for significance not success. I feel as women we often concentrate our efforts on achieving material success or climbing the corporate ladder and do not place nearly as much effort on the contributions we make to humanity and in our relationships with one another.*

*Women need to support each other and help each other succeed. Don't forget that old adage 'You also gleam when you cause another's star to shine.'"*

—Hazel McCallion

# Erin Pizzey

## Founder of shelters for battered women and children, England

Today we take for granted that there are women's shelters across the globe where abused women and children have a safe haven. Yet it was ERIN PIZZEY's bold and innovative vision that resulted in the establishment of the world's first domestic violence shelter in Chiswick, England in 1971. Even if she didn't discover domestic violence, she was the person who forced it to the forefront as a major social problem.

Erin was born in China in 1939, the daughter of a diplomat. She was captured by the Japanese during the Second World War, held hostage, exchanged for Japanese prisoners, and then put on the last boat out of Shanghai. She has lived in Persia (now Iran), Beirut, Singapore, New Mexico, the Cayman Islands, Tuscany and now Twickenham in England.

She wrote the first book to truly tackle the issue of domestic violence titled *Scream Quietly or the Neighbors Will Hear*, which was turned into a 1979 film aired on PBS. Erin also became the resident expert on family violence on the popular Phil Donahue talk show.

Erin and her family received death threats after the 1982 publication of her book *Prone to Violence*, wherein she suggested that domestic violence was a multi-faceted issue and was not always perpetrated by men on women. At the time this was somewhat revolutionary thinking. It was around this time that she moved from England to North America.

When she was finished with her non-fiction writing, she turned to penning fiction, writing a dozen novels. She has also contributed to many international journals and newspapers, such as the Sunday Times and Cosmopolitan.

Erin is still active in the women's shelter movement, and recently acted as an advisor to the Aisha Yateem Family Counseling Centre, the first women and children refuge in Bahrain.

She has been recognized with several awards including: the Diploma of Honor by the International Order of Volunteers for Peace, the Nancy Astor

Award for Journalism, the Distinguished Leader Award from the World Congress of Victimology, and the St. Valentino Palm d'Oro International Award for Literature.

Erin is a refreshingly outspoken woman, who tells it like she sees it and continuously attempts to represent the under-represented.

And when she's not out helping others you might just hear her playing the violin.

*"When I was young my mentor said:*
*'Erin, always do better than your best.'"*
—Erin Pizzey

Courtesy of Erin Pizzey

# Angela Salinas

## Brigadier General, United States Marine Corps, USA

Brigadier General ANGELA SALINAS is the commanding general of the Marine Corps Recruit Depot in San Diego; the first Hispanic female to become a United States Marine Corps (USMC) general officer, and the sixth female in the Marine Corps to reach the rank of Brigadier General. She was probably not what the USMC originally had envisioned when many years ago they had coined a recruiting slogan of needing "A Few Good Men."

She was born in Alice, Texas, the youngest of five children. In the early 60's her family moved to northern California. Her decision to join the Marine Corps came during her sophomore year at the Dominican College of San Rafael where she was studying history. Angie went to mail a letter at the local post office and a Marine recruiter who was there asked her why she wasn't a Marine? She enlisted four days later and within a week was on her way to the Marine Corps Recruit Depot. Angie then returned to college to obtain her Bachelor's degree in history and eventually went on to obtain a Master's degree from the Naval War College.

She has commanded at every rank in the Marines. In June 1989, Brigadier General Salinas assumed command of Recruiting Station Charleston and became the first woman in the history of the Marine Corps to command a recruiting station. In June 1992, she became the first woman assigned as a combat service support ground monitor responsible for the assignments of over 1,000 senior officers. She was the first female appointed as a plans and policy officer for a major combatant command in 1999 and in May 2001, when she assumed command of the 12th Marine Corps District, became the first woman to serve as a recruiting district commanding officer. She is the first woman to command the Marine Corps Recruit Depot/Western Recruiting Region in San Diego.

The list of her personal decorations is long and includes not only recognition from the Marines in the form of the Defense Superior Service Medal, the

Legion of Merit with gold star, the Meritorious Service Medal with 2 gold stars, and others, but also Meritorious Service Awards from the Federal Employed Women, the National Image and Latina Style Magazine to name a few. She has received recognition for her leadership by the Navy League and has been named as one of the top 100 influential Hispanics in the US and as one of the 80 most elite women.

Courtesy of the USMC

She attributes her success to her 93 year old mother who has lived with her since she was a young lieutenant and her sister Janie who had done it all long before women knew they could do it all.

Brigadier General Angie Salinas has also shown that she can do it all. Fortunately for everyone, that day many years ago, Angie needed to mail a letter.

*"If you love what you do you will never work a day in your life!"*
—*Brigadier General Angela Salinas*

97

# Sima Samar

## Chairperson, Afghanistan Independent Human Rights Commission, Afghanistan

When Dr. SIMA SAMAR was born in 1957 in Afghanistan, she seemed to have the odds stacked against her, as both a woman and as a Hazara, one of the most persecuted minorities in the country. Yet it's exactly these circumstances that caused her to put both her life and liberty at risk, as she has continually striven to be a voice for the disenfranchised.

Sima received a medical degree in 1982 from Kabul University, a career chosen based on her desire to make a positive difference in her country. Yet her work to effect positive change in Afghanistan was performed for many years from Pakistan, where she fled after her husband was arrested during the Russian invasion of Afghanistan. He was one of more than 500 educated people rounded up one night in 1984, never to be heard from again.

During her 17 years in Pakistan she became a leader for educating Afghan women and girls. Sima founded The Shuhada Organization, which now operates 55 schools for girls and boys in Afghanistan and 3 schools for Afghan refugees in Quetta, Pakistan. During the Taliban regime, Shuhada's schools in Central Afghanistan were among the few academic girls' primary schools and the organization's girls' high schools were the only high schools that girls were able to attend in the country. The Shuhada Organization also ran underground home school classes for girls in Kabul. Following the collapse of the Taliban, these home school classes became the basis for two above ground schools for girls that now teach 800 students.

Dr. Samar is currently the Chairwoman of the Independent Afghanistan Human Rights Commission. In this position, she oversees the conduct of human rights education programs across Afghanistan, the implementation of a nationwide women's rights education program, and the monitoring and investigation of human rights abuses across the country. Dr. Samar convened the Commission, which is the first Human Rights Commission in Afghanistan's history.

From December 22, 2001 until June 22, 2002, Dr. Sima Samar served as the Deputy Chair and Minister of Women's Affairs for the Interim Administration of Afghanistan. Dr. Samar was one of only two women cabinet ministers in the Interim Administration of Afghanistan's government.

During this Administration, Sima established the first-ever Afghanistan Ministry of Women's Affairs. Among other accomplishments, the Ministry won the right of women government employees to return to their jobs and to keep their seniority, oversaw the re-entry of girls to schools, launched a women's rights legal department, and opened a school for married girls offering tailoring, literacy, and embroidery courses at the Ministry's headquarters.

She has been recognized for her leadership and courage by dozens of human and women's rights organizations globally, and continues her work in Afghanistan and also as the United Nations special envoy to Darfur, Sudan.

Sima has paid a heavy price for her commitment on a personal level. Yet despite the difficulties she is happy with the work she does. She has said that her work may be only a drop in the ocean, but at least she feels that that drop is something positive.

Courtesy of Dr. Sima Samar

*"Build your capacity and self confidence—everything is possible. It might be difficult, but not impossible."*
—Dr. Sima Samar

99

# Dame Catherine Tizard
## ONZ, GCMG, GCVO, DBE, QSO

## 16th Governor General, New Zealand

When drawn to a life in public service, some people find a way to live out that desire, regardless of their circumstances. Dame CATHERINE TIZARD was one of those individuals long before she was appointed to the role of Governor General of New Zealand.

The only child of Scottish immigrants, she was born Catherine Anne Maclean on April 4, 1931, in Auckland. She went to Auckland University in 1949 and it was there she met Bob Tizard who would one day become New Zealand's Deputy Prime Minister. The two were married in 1951, had four children but divorced 30 years later.

Dame Catherine's first administrative role came when she joined the Play Centre Committee of which she later became president. She was then elected to the Board of Governors of the Eastern Suburbs Secondary Schools.

She returned to university to finish a degree in zoology in 1961. The next year she became a part-time tutor in this discipline, which eventually resulted in a tenured appointment.

After spending twenty years concentrating on her family and teaching, Dame Catherine refocused her energy and began her political career. She was elected to the Auckland City Council in 1971 and remained a city councillor for 12 years while still tutoring at Auckland University.

Dame Catherine was elected Mayor of Auckland in 1983, the first woman to hold that position and remained in the post for seven years . During her time in office she received the title of DBE (Dame Commander of the Order of the British Empire).

In 1990 Dame Catherine Tizard added another item to her list of 'firsts' when Queen Elizabeth II appointed her the first female Governor-General of New Zealand. It was fitting that the 100th anniversary of Women's Suffrage in New Zealand occurred during her term.

Dame Catherine has an extremely long list of organizations for which she is or has been a Patron or Trustee and her list of honors and titles is equally as extensive. Besides the honor of DBE, she also was bestowed with the Dame Grand Cross of the Royal Victorian Order in 1990. In 2002, Dame Catherine received the rare honor of being made a member of the Order of New Zealand.

Even in retirement Dame Catherine has remained a significant political force in New Zealand. In 2004 she became a member of an organization which promoted the idea of holding a national referendum to determine if New Zealand's flag should be changed. A key aspect of the committee is also mirrored in Dame Catherine's life and career, namely that the prime motive was to determine what the people thought and wanted and to act upon that. As Dame Catherine explained, "Our present flag served a young, post-colonial country well, but the time has come to consider a change which more appropriately recognizes our changed identity and confidence in ourselves."

By changing just a few words this comment can apply perfectly to Dame Catherine herself as she continually adapts to better serve the needs of those around her.

*"I have always remembered a quotation from the famous English author Aldous Huxley—he who wrote The Brave New World— who was widely regarded as a profound thinker and philosopher— a font of wisdom, in fact. In his latter years he was asked many times what advice he had for people—what he had learned from his lifetime of thinking, studying and writing.*

*I would like to use this as my 'one piece of advice': 'It is a bit embarrassing to have been concerned with the human problem all one's life and find at the end, that one has no more to offer by way of advice than 'Try to be a little kinder.'"*

—Dame Catherine Tizard

Marye Anne Fox
*USA*

Joan
Stringer
*Scotland*

# In the Pursuit of Knowledge

Lucija Čok
*Slovenia*

Universities provide opportunities not only for learning and understanding, they also provide the world with individuals that find cures, write literature, create scientific understanding, lead countries, treat the ill, enact the law and a myriad of other profound contributions.

In this section we are highlighting women who have, or who are leading, universities, facilitating a better future through education. Their intense commitment to society's betterment through knowledge is evident in their stories.

Education is a universal pursuit as evidenced by the different geographies represented by these educators.

# Lucija Čok

## Former Rector, University of Primorska, Slovenia

Dr. LUCIJA ČOK was the first Rector of the University of Primorksa and the first woman to serve as Rector of a university in Slovenia. The University of Primorska was established in 2003 as the third university in the country.

She is a senior research scientist in the field of early multilingualism and an associate professor of didactics of multilingualism and intercultural communication at the University.

From 2000 to 2002 she was a member of the Slovenian government and was appointed the Minister of Education, Science and Sport. Dr. Čok has a passion for education and has contributed significantly to the establishment of higher education institutions in the Slovene region of Primorska, as well as to the expansion of the Slovene higher education network.

Her academic research is primarily focused on phenomena related to languages and cultures in contact areas, as well as to education that encourages peaceful co-existence of various cultures and ethnic groups.

The findings of Dr. Čok's research have been published in several languages and she has lectured at many international universities. She has headed and coordinated national and international projects in the fields of didactics of foreign languages, early multilingualism and intercultural communication.

She has received awards from the President of France and the President of Italy for her promotion of languages and strategies for the encouragement of linguistic diversity.

Dr. Čok is also collaborating with European Commission expert panels that form linguistic policies and strategies for the reform of higher education and research.

*"The woman leader has to be different. It is wrong if a woman, as a leader, tries to adopt a man's leadership style, or if both of them are trying to change one another, believing that his/her own style is the only option.*

*The 'acting' style of decision makers is an important factor in their success. In cases where the decision maker is a woman, her genetics, her temper and gender give her some advantages, such as tolerance in accepting 'otherness,' perseverance, readiness to achieve the goal and diligence.*

*The stereotypes and the traditional perception of her role in society; prejudices and lack of acceptance of her authority within the group where she is 'acting' are serious obstacles to her leadership.*

*Men and women can learn from one another and with learning and teaching each other make the world better."*
—Dr. Lucija Čok

Courtesy of Lucija Čok

# Marye Anne Fox

## Chemist, University Chancellor, USA

MARYE ANNE FOX knows about time management. With three sons, two stepsons and a demanding career, she often found herself dictating letters during little league games, trying to balance family and career demands.

After receiving her PhD in physical organic chemistry from Dartmouth College, she spent 22 years at the University of Texas where she advanced from assistant professor of organic chemistry to vice president for research. Marye Anne left Texas to become the first female chief executive of North Carolina State University in 1998 and remained there until her appointment as the Chancellor of the University of California in San Diego in 2004.

She has expanded her influence well beyond her roles at the three universities. She served as a science advisor to George W. Bush during his tenure as Governor of Texas, and currently sits on the President's Council of Advisors on Science and Technology. She has been awarded eight honorary degrees and her CV lists pages of research, public service and teaching awards from organizations in the U.S. and internationally.

Marye Anne is passionate about public education, which she believes in the U.S. is an "endangered species." She believes strongly about ensuring that all students have access to affordable, high quality education and that if the quality in public institutions declines, so will the opportunity to take advantage of what she sees as the United States advantage—its diversity.

She grew up in Canton, Ohio and has noted that "if you were intelligent at all, then you thought about science." Well, Marye Anne did more than think about it when she fell in love with chemistry and had the self-confidence to pursue a career in a highly male-dominated field.

Hanging on her wall is an exercise which the young Marye Anne did when she was learning to write the letter "W." It says "You Must Wish and Work," the characteristics that she believes are common in all successful people.

*"Recognize that success requires both perseverance and adaptability and that they are not inherently contradictory."*
—Marye Anne Fox

Courtesy of Marye Anne Fox

# Joan Stringer, CBE

## Principal and Vice Chancellor Napier University, Scotland

People often have the notion that for a woman to succeed in business, politics, government, or in whatever her chosen field may be, she must be aggressive, even cut-throat. While that may apply to some, it definitely does not describe the highly talented and immensely successful Professor JOAN STRINGER. Certainly not lacking in ambition, she has taken all of her zeal and drive and focused them, not on her own career, but rather on her ultimate passion—to improve education in Scotland.

Professor Joan Stringer was never one to miss an opportunity to further her goal. Take for example her challenging role as an instructor to a diverse group of adult males who spanned the full range of intellectual capabilities and socio-economical origins. Not overly remarkable? Think again—the classes were taught to male convicts in a prison!

While most of her credentials are not as colorful as the one just mentioned, Joan has amassed an extremely impressive list of accomplishments. She began her career in education in 1980 as a lecturer in public administration, and then obtained her PhD investigating the effectiveness of industrial training policy in Britain.

She is known as one of Scotland's most influential women in the field of education, having been the first female to be appointed head of a university in her country. She sits on a wide range of committees intended to improve the quality of education, including representing Scotland on the UK Committee of Inquiry into Higher Education.

In 2001 Professor Stringer was honored with a CBE (Companion of the British Empire), an award presented to her at Buckingham Palace. She had come a long way from her humble beginnings. Having been born to a working class family, Joan initially left academic pursuits to study art and graphic design. At the age of twenty four, after spending years accumulating the required prerequisite credits, she enrolled full time in university. It was no doubt this experience influenced her career path. She has always maintained that intelligent, talented people come from all walks of life and therefore quality education should be available to everyone, not just to the wealthy.

Earlier in her career, Professor Stringer, then principal of the Queen Margaret University College, made the decision to grow and develop the institution rather than to merge with another. Today Queen Margaret University is flourishing.

As the Principal and Vice Chancellor of Napier University, Professor Stringer has made it her mission to tap into the unrealized potential of her university. She is a tireless promoter of her institution and is determined to solidify the reputation of Napier as an institution which is focused on helping businesses solve their problems by producing highly qualified graduates. She is also actively developing connections with universities in other countries, particularly in China, where Napier is affiliated with over twenty universities—more than any other university in the United Kingdom.

Courtesy of Joan Stringer

The keys to her success lie in her collaborative approach and in her communication skills. In characteristic style Joan works with her colleagues and staff members, encouraging them to become confident, independent thinkers and to believe in themselves. The results speak volumes.

*"The most important advice I can give is to always believe in yourself, stay focused on your goals, but also on your achievements. You must be tenacious to be successful, so if you know you can achieve something don't hesitate—go for it."*
—Professor Joan Stringer

# 1 Piece of Advice—Summary

"Learn to say 'NO!'"

Olga Abramova, *Former Deputy of the Belarussian Government, Belarus [p74]*

"Every day is a new start. It's never too late to change, correct, improve, apologize or expand your horizons. Live for now and without regrets."

Val Ackerman, *President USA Basketball, USA [p2]*

"Don't listen to any advice that will stop you from following your dreams."

Evelyne Aiello, *Conductor, France [p44]*

"My advice to women is to emphasize networking. Having good relations with influential individuals, and senior officials in organizations in different countries has enabled me to obtain crucial information, gain insight on new investment opportunities, and secure deals.

These relations have also helped me place our products and services in addition to launching myself and Global Investment House 'Global' in the financial world. A significant network of relations is a prelude to prominence; not having one will make you a soldier, but never a general."

Maha AlGhunaim, *Chairperson and Managing Director Global Investment House, Kuwait [p4]*

**"Take responsibility for your own career:** Early in my career, I was passed over for a promotion. I went to my boss and shared with him a list of my accomplishments. He didn't know that I had done all of those things. The lesson—don't assume that the people you work for are aware of all the 'good work' that you are doing. Find a way to let them know without being a braggart.

**Have a Mentor and be a Mentor:** Having a mentor—or, in my case, a number of mentors—was absolutely critical in shaping my career. A good mentor cares about you as a person, is interested in your success and provides a perspective you may not have considered. And don't forget that it goes both ways. Along with finding a mentor, be a mentor. Help others along the way, and you will feel more rewarded in your career.

**Seek balance to do what's right:** How you act on your values determines your reputation and, ultimately, your success. But if you're totally dependent on your career for personal fulfillment, you may be tempted to cut corners if things go awry. Maintaining the proper balance in your life helps you to do what's right. By keeping your work in perspective and staying true to your personal values, you can maintain the strength of your convictions."

Sharon Allen, *Chairman, Deloitte LLP, USA [p6]*

"My secret in life has been first, to believe in myself, my ability to perform. Secondly and with God's help, I have moved forward to accomplish my goals. This has not been easy and there have been many hurdles on the way, but the fact that I have come this far is testimony that it can be done and in fact, it has been done. Women must strive to achieve their set goals. It comes from within oneself—it is never given on a silver platter."

Lady Justice Joyce Aluoch, *Judge, Court of Appeal, Kenya [p76]*

"When in a leadership role—be yourself! You don't need to change your style to emulate somebody else. Your own style is the most effective way to promote change within your own personal life and career."

Kim Baird, *Chief of the Tsawwassen First Nation, Canada [p78]*

"Never take a job for the pay or title—take it only because you have a passion for the cause to which the company or organization is dedicated. Then it just doesn't feel like work and you will find that success is easily attained because you are completely committed to what you're doing."

Colleen Barrett, *President Emeritus, Southwest Airlines, USA [p8]*

"If I can give only one piece of advice to young business women, I want to pass on what someone told me when I was starting out. I have never forgotten it, because it is advice that has served me so well through my years as Minister of Culture and as CEO of TVOntario, and I hope it will do the same for you.

It's very simple really. When you start something, settle on three objectives you want to achieve. Having thoughtfully established this course of action, do not allow yourself to be sidetracked by the many other worthwhile things you may wish to do, or be pressured by others to do. Work continually towards your goals. Even though you may face challenges along the way, your three objectives will be like beacons and guide you on your journey to success."

Isabel Bassett, *Author, Broadcaster, Politician, Philanthropist, Canada [p10]*

"Every woman, at any point in her life, has a platform. It may be the job you have; it may be your role in the community or even in your family. It looks different at different times, at different stages and depends on many things. But we all have one.

The Rutgers women's basketball team used their platform as collegiate student athletes to speak out about an injustice which had a powerful impact on our nation and its values.

Successful women use their platform all through their life to affect and lead those around them to a better place, bringing about positive change. Think about what you do in your life and always be sure you are truly using the platform you have to make a difference…however big or small."

Beth Brooke, *Global Vice Chair, Ernst and Young, USA [p12]*

"I used to hate the word 'ambition' because in my mind, I saw it as Blind Ambition. I came to realize that ambition means being willing to step outside of your comfort zone. It means taking a leap of faith, stepping up to a challenge, and living your values. So, with integrity, be ambitious! Raise the bar and deliver more than others think is possible!"

Adriane M. Brown, *President and CEO, Honeywell Transportation Systems, USA [p16]*

"The woman leader has to be different. It is wrong if a woman, as a leader, tries to adopt a man's leadership style, or if both of them are trying to change one another, believing that his/her own style is the only option.

The 'acting' style of decision makers is an important factor in their success. In cases where the decision maker is a woman, her genetics, her temper and gender give her some advantages, such as tolerance in accepting 'otherness,' perseverance, readiness to achieve the goal and diligence.

The stereotypes and the traditional perception of her role in society; prejudices and lack of acceptance of her authority within the group where she is 'acting' are serious obstacles to her leadership.

Men and women can learn from one another and with learning and teaching each other make the world better."

Lucija Čok, *Former Rector, University of Primorska, Slovenia [p104]*

"First of all, never forget that you are unique! Whatever your goal in life might be, it is always worthwhile. It is always worth fighting for your opinions and your personal freedom. Never doubt, just do it! There is something, a talent or a gift, which you have and nobody else possesses and it is your duty to discover it and to make it real. This will surely lead to a happy and fulfilling life."

Barbara Dennerlein, *Jazz Organist, Composer, Arranger, Germany [p46]*

"Throw yourself completely into the task that's to hand and possibilities will emerge that you could never have imagined."

Alison Elliot, *Former Moderator, Church of Scotland, Scotland [p36]*

"My advice is very simple: pick a small number of things and do them well. Be ruthless, throw out all unnecessary things. You can do one thing well, probably two, but maybe not three and certainly not four. Examples of 'things': scientific researcher, spouse, mother, community worker, teacher, public speaker, fundraiser, popular writer. Choose, focus and go for it!"

Sandra Faber, *Professor, Researcher—Astronomy, Astrophysics, USA [p66]*

"Recognize that success requires both perseverance and adaptability and that they are not inherently contradictory."

Marye Anne Fox, *Chemist, University Chancellor, USA [p106]*

"**Plan**—your life. Equip yourself with the best possible education. You may or may not meet 'Mr. Right.' You may or may not have a family. One day you may be alone and may be responsible for more people than yourself—i.e., your children, your parents.

**Trust**—your instincts, your gut feeling. You know when something feels right and when it does not.

**Believe**—in love, in dreams, in wonders, in magic but first and foremost, believe in yourself.

**Listen**—out of respect for others and because you can always learn something.

**Have a Life**—nurture friendships, start a hobby, read (books), write (by hand)."

Claudia Fritsche, *Ambassador of the Principality of Liechtenstein to the USA [p80]*

"Many years ago when I was going through a difficult time I was talking to someone who mentored both me and Stella Rimmington. I asked him how on earth she (Stella) coped with everything thrown at her. He said they had discussed that only the previous day.

She said that she knew that all the problems thrown at her would be thrown at whoever sat in the same chair—they are issues that go with the territory and not personally directed.

'Don't take it personally' has been the mantra I have lived by at work ever since—and it has been invaluable in keeping me sane, focused and relatively level headed!"

Thanks Stella!

Jayne-Anne Gadhia, *CEO, Virgin Money, England [p18]*

"Be true to yourself."

Dame Evelyn Glennie, *Solo Percussionist, England [p48]*

"My piece of advice is to find some kind of work you can do real good, get satisfaction from and be so good at it that people will pay you to do it! Doesn't have to be 'fancy' work like writing or acting or singing; not even being great with numbers or persuasion. If this satisfying work gets you out of bed every day and on to its pursuit; if you get valued for it and paid for it, you can be a pretty happy person.

After I'd been a secretary since 16 and had 17 secretarial jobs, I got to be 33 and started writing advertising copy. I got the job because I wrote good letters to my boss, the head of the agency, so he let me switch to something more creative.

If you're good with food, I think you could go work in a restaurant as a hostess or maybe start a catering service from your home. I just find that getting up to go to a job where they need you is a wonderfully satisfying thing to do.

At age 86, I work for a wonderful company, which appreciates the money made from a magazine I edited for many years and so they let me continue to have a job and get paid.

Repeat: the work doesn't have to be so-called important or attention grabbing, just something you do well that helps other people, brings satisfaction and self respect to you and brings in a little money…enough to live on or more!"

Helen Gurley Brown, *Author, Editor-in-Chief, Cosmopolitan Magazine, USA [p14]*

"Timing may not always be the best, however when opportunity knocks, open the door with confidence and walk straight through!"

Joanne Hayes-White, *Chief, San Francisco Fire Department, USA [p82]*

"Be passionate—love what you do! We spend more time at work than anywhere else. It is essential to your success, fulfillment, and happiness that you enjoy your colleagues and are passionate about what you do."

Susan M. Ivey, *Chair, President and CEO Reynolds America, USA [p20]*

"One of the most important pieces of advice I can give to women I wrote in my book *Find Where the Wind Goes*, and the advice is this: Pay attention to learn from all the adventures you've had in life, big and small, for within each, there is valuable insight to help you throughout life. The lessons that happen when satisfying our curiosity, but which appear to conflict with maintaining our dignity, are particularly important."

Mae Jemison, *Astronaut, Entrepreneur, Physician, Engineer, Dancer, USA [p68]*

"Be generous of spirit—even in adversity and when under assault."

Suzanne Nora Johnson, *Former Vice Chairman, Senior Director, Goldman Sachs, USA [p22]*

"My advice to women is to develop strong will-power, self-knowledge and recognize the grace of God in what they do."

Anna Jokai, *Author, Hungary [p50]*

"Life is short, try to savour every moment."

Karen Kain, *Artistic Director, National Ballet of Canada,*
*Former Prima Ballerina, Canada [p52]*

"There is always something good in the problems and
obstacles you face. Look for it!"

Yolanda Kakabadse Navarro, *Environmentalist, Ecuador [p84]*

"Tell the truth. Tell the absolute truth.
Sometimes it is hard to be both truthful and kind.
But it is always possible to find
a way to be both.

Make sure someone else knows what you know.
As a lawyer in the Pentagon told me when I first arrived:
'Do not have secrets.'

Even when I have thought the truth was difficult or did not reflect
well on me, it always proved to have been a wise choice to have
told the truth and to have had no secrets."

Claudia J. Kennedy, *Lieutenant General US Army (Retired), USA [p86]*

"Never Give Up!"

Neelie Kroes, *European Commissioner for Competition, Belgium [p88]*

"In life, one needs to learn to look beyond the constraints of the moment and dedicate one's energies to doing one's best during trying times. This is how one can position oneself, little by little to take advantage of the opportunities of the future when these present themselves."

Dame Calliopa Pearlette Louisy, *Governor General, St. Lucia [p90]*

"Take on challenges with a sense of purpose. Success comes to those who own problems, not tasks. Solving problems generates a tremendous sense of confidence and satisfaction. It is this approach that has helped me become a successful entrepreneur. This problem solving ethos is strongly engrained in our HR practices. I truly believe that this approach can make ordinary people do extra-ordinary things."

Kiran Mazumdar-Shaw, *Chair Biocon, Entrepreneur, Scientist, India [p24]*

"I consider it a blessing to have a job that I love. Having a life filled with meaning and purpose and living my life in a Christian-like manner helps to motivate me and keep me energized.

In this vein, my advice to women would be to strive for significance not success. I feel as women we often concentrate our efforts on achieving material success or climbing the corporate ladder and do not place nearly as much effort on the contributions we make to humanity and in our relationships with one another.

Women need to support each other and help each other succeed. Don't forget that old adage 'You also gleam when you cause another's star to shine.'"

Hazel McCallion, *Mayor, Canada [p92]*

"Question everything around you and trust your inner instincts."
Deepa Mehta, *Director, Producer, Screenwriter, Canada & India [p54]*

"If a woman wants to make a living in a profession such as
conducting, which has traditionally been a male bastion,
she has to be better professionally prepared than any man.
Then she has to find a way which is consistent, but not offensive.
Till now this has worked for me!"
Miriam Němcová, *Conductor, Czech Republic [p56]*

"Never act when angry—*always* wait till you've cooled down."
Baroness Julia Neuberger, *Rabbi, Author, Social Reformer, England [p38]*

"Understand that, as a woman, the most significant thing that you can
do in life is to find your own purpose. Having found that purpose,
your mission is to pursue it with all the passion and courage that you
can find within yourself. You are not alone as women everywhere
grow in resolve towards the common purpose of freedom and equity
for women across the globe, and you will find that the whole universe
celebrates your sound and will make way for your success!"
Blossom O'Meally Nelson, *Business Executive, Educator, Environmentalist,
Jamaica [p26]*

"When I was young my mentor said:
'Erin, always do better than your best.'"
Erin Pizzey, *Founder of shelters for battered women and children, England [p94]*

"What has always worked for me—whatever I'm doing, thinking, feeling wondering—I put a little God in there."

Della Reese, *Singer, Actress, Entertainer, Author, Minister USA [p58]*

"Believe in yourself and your aspirations.
Don't let doubts or naysayers stop you from reaching your dreams.
The only difference between those who do, and those who don't is that those who do—do!"

Heather Reisman, *CEO and Founder, Indigo Books & Music, Canada [p28]*

"If you love what you do you will never work a day in your life!"

Angela Salinas, *Brigadier General, United States Marine Corps, USA [p96]*

"Build your capacity and self confidence—everything is possible.
It might be difficult, but not impossible."

Sima Samar, *Chairperson, Afghanistan Independent Human Rights Commission, Afghanistan [p98]*

"The most important advice I can give is to always believe in yourself, stay focused on your goals, but also on your achievements. You must be tenacious to be successful, so if you know you can achieve something don't hesitate—go for it."

Joan Stringer, *Principal and Vice Chancellor Napier University, Scotland [p108]*

"Don't believe anyone that tells you that you can't excel at two things at once. I've followed two passions in my life and have had twice the happiness."

Genevieve Thiers, *CEO Sittercity, Opera Singer, USA [p30]*

"As I found out this year, there is nothing quite like turning 50 to propel 'philosopher' to the top of your resume. Now that I'm a card carrying member of the 'sage and wise' club, I shake my head at the staggering amount of time and energy—two of my most precious resources—that I wasted on 'worrying.' Now that I have the benefit of a few years of perspective tucked under my ever-expanding belt, I can say with assurance that 'worry' is women's worst enemy. Reflecting over the last 50 years, I see an interesting pattern emerge; when I get out of my own way, release the worry, things generally work out much better.

As Mark Twain once astutely remarked, 'I am an old man and have known a great many troubles, but most of them never happened.' Don't wait until you're 50 to finally put worry in its proper place; six feet under the compost pile."

Joanne Thomas Yaccato, *Entrepreneur, Author, Women's Advocate, Canada [p32]*

"I have always remembered a quotation from the famous English author Aldous Huxley—he who wrote *The Brave New World*—who was widely regarded as a profound thinker and philosopher—a font of wisdom, in fact. In his latter years he was asked many times what advice he had for people—what he had learned from his lifetime of thinking, studying and writing. I would like to use this as my 'one piece of advice': It is a bit embarrassing to have been concerned with the human problem all one's life and find at the end, that one has no more to offer by way of advice than 'Try to be a little kinder.'"

Dame Catherine Tizard, *16ᵗʰ Governor General, New Zealand [p100]*

"Decide what your priorities are. If your first priority is to promote women's rights, you need to act on that and realize that this will probably have consequences for your career. If your first priority is your career, you will promote women's rights by who you are and by what you do in that career. In this case, being a shining example in a leadership role is the best thing you can do to forward the cause of women in today's world."

The Right Reverend Ann Tottenham, *Anglican Church Bishop, Canada [p40]*

"People talk a lot about 'passion' and while 'passion' is an important component of leading a full life, I think it's an overused and under explained word. For me it means that a person should follow the path that makes them happy. People might tell you to follow another path—go to a certain school or college; take a certain job, etc.,—and it might be easier to do what you are told, what has been prescribed for you, but if you are not happy or don't feel right about going in that direction then you'll never find what 'passion' really means.

Passion means that you, before anyone else, have to be happy with your choices. If you are not happy in your life then you will not be able to make anyone else happy—your children, your husband, your friends.

So the one piece of advice I would give is to follow the path that makes you happiest, that feels right. Trust your intuition to guide you and dig deep into your soul and listen to yourself and what your heart tells you, and have faith that the future is inside of you. Then you can create the energy to make whatever it is you want happen."

Patty Wagstaff, *Champion Aerobatic Pilot, USA [p70]*

"My parents taught me through deed, not just word, perhaps the single most important of life's lessons—and it's my shorthand, not their's—but the message was clear:

### Character Trumps Genius

Simply put, you can be smart, but if you are not kind and decent, fair and generous—when it is difficult to do so—then all the brains in the world are for naught."

Pamela D. Wallin, *Journalist, TV Host, Diplomat, Entrepreneur, Author, Canada [p62]*

# About the Authors

# Patricia J. Moser-Stern

Patricia grew up a "tom-boy" choosing trucks over dolls, and judo over ballet. This attitude has followed her through life, as her parents always encouraged her to look at barriers as obstacles to be overcome. She was and is an "achiever," who sets a goal and then makes it happen, through sheer force of will.

Her educational path was determined by pursuit of subjects that she loved, so she ended up with an eclectic mix of a BSc. in Psychology, a BSc. in Chemistry, and an M.B.A. During her tenure in university, the classes were never enough to keep her occupied, so Patricia became a Reporter and News and Entertainment Editor of a student newspaper; a championship debater and the President of the Debating Society; a writer for the Administration newspaper; and in her spare time she taught Marketing courses at the Undergraduate level and ran the University's Speakers Program.

She began her career in a biologics company, where she took a role in the Production part of the organization—hardly a female friendly pursuit. She learned a lot about the perception of women at this company and about the "dance" at which women need to be much more astute than their male counterparts. Patricia then pursued, not only different roles, in different organizations, but in completely different industries, satisfying her need to continually learn and challenge the status quo.

Patricia has had great success as both a corporate executive and entrepreneur. She is recognized as a thought leader, visionary, innovator, and change leader, who continuously challenges organizations to conquer their fears and take the leap of faith that will create new and exciting realities. Publications have sought out her opinions and recognized her achievements, and she has written about and presented on many topics throughout North America and abroad.

From early on in her career, to the present day, Patricia has considered it a responsibility (as well as a pleasure) to provide direction and inspiration to women who were trying to define themselves in their career and life path. She's served on the Board of an association focused on women entrepreneurs; she's spoken at women's organization events; and she was and is always sought out by women, who are looking to Patricia for her *1 Piece of Advice*™.

Patricia is a true leader and an impassioned advocate for women's rights. She is sought out by magazines and conferences for her prolific writing and presenting capabilities, respectively. Her ability to create the possible out of what others believe to be impossible will ensure that *1 Piece of Advice*™ becomes not only a reality, but an inspirational best seller for women around the world.

She lives in the Toronto area in Canada with her husband and son.

Patricia's *1 Piece of Advice*™?

*"Dream BIG, otherwise you will only achieve small!"*

# About the Authors

# Barbara K. Moser

For Barbara, her academic pursuits, her career, her passions and interests have been an extension of those she developed in her childhood. She spent the first ten years of her life in a rural setting in a family dominated by men. As the youngest child and only female Barbara learned early that if you wanted to play at all, you had to do "boy things" and play by the "boy rules." You had to be able to run faster, hit the ball further, and climb higher to prove your worth. If you got hurt, you got on with it and above all, you never showed fear—you felt it, but you never showed it.

Barbara excelled in maths and sciences which led her to obtain a degree in Mechanical Engineering from the University of Toronto. Yet she has always had a keen interest in the "arts" related subjects. Her high school English teacher was shocked when Barbara, the avid reader and writer, announced she was pursuing a career in science and stated "Good luck studying sciences with your 'artsie' mind!" which became somewhat of Barbara's mantra.

In her academic career, Barbara solved the same difficult problems, as her overwhelmingly male classmates, yet she seemed to do so by a different route. This dichotomy was further evidenced by the fact that she was one of the very few (if not only) Engineering students who minored in psychology and took courses such as languages, philosophy and religion as electives.

As Barbara began her engineering career, she developed a passion for operations management and the Quality field. Moreover, she also discovered her fascination with those mechanical things that fly (aka airplanes).

While working and having two toddlers at home, Barbara decided that with her free time, which was relatively non-existent, she would pursue an M.B.A. in the evenings.

Her career advanced with this additional degree, and she became very successful in her professional career, as she grew a large manufacturing organization to over twice the output in a short period of time while keeping costs down and greatly improving efficiencies. All the while she was always surrounded by a majority of male colleagues, not unlike her childhood experience.

Barbara has always been active in the community, spending countless hours on her volunteer work while raising, together with her husband, three wonderful children. A few years ago, Barbara obtained her private pilot's license, taking her love of airplanes to the next level. It was her personal refresher course in mastering fear, tackling obstacles and acquiring a new skill. Barbara began lecturing to girls in high school, early in her career, about the importance of taking math and science courses. She also gave seminars for young women on behalf of the professional engineers' society to encourage them to consider a career in engineering. For a time she took a sabbatical from corporate life and taught sciences and business subjects in high school. She has also chaired a professional society and was editor (and chief contributor) of the society's newsletter.

Just like Patricia, Barbara is an impassioned advocate of women's rights, and has been sought out to provide her own *1 Piece of Advice*™ to women throughout her work life, particularly as she has chosen an atypical career for a woman. She focuses on the possibilities and is looking forward to ensuring that *1 Piece of Advice*™ reaches a broad audience of women, which will inspire them and which will keep them moving forward, through the hardships and obstacles that are faced in their life's journey.

Barbara's *1 Piece of Advice*™?

*"The words of the poet Tennyson, 'I am a part of all that I have met,' have always resonated with me. I believe we must all strive to find meaning in those encounters and experiences, positive or negative, for they have made us who we are."*

# Acknowledgements

The journey in creating this book has been an amazing experience. However, as with many things in life it could not have been done without the generosity of others.

We are very grateful to all of the following people who have provided their wisdom and support:

- The wonderful women who responded to our request without hesitation;
- Richard Ebbs, who provided us with ideas and eventually the photo which adorns the cover and Anne de Haas whose photographic mastery is evident in the authors' photos;
- Anne Willems, otherwise known as "eagle eye," who did a lot of the proofing of the text;
- Susan Foran who provided us with her expert legal and business advice;
- The two Bills (Fontaine and Hushion) from White Knight Distribution, who helped to educate two publishing novices and provided a lot of humor in the process;
- Fortunato Aglialoro our magnificent book designer who has creativity, humor and patience wrapped up in one package.

And finally to our families: Allen Stern and Christopher (Patricia's husband and son); and Dennis, Beth, Katie and Thomas Pyle (Barbara's husband and children), whose unwavering belief and unconditional support and love help us get through each and every day.

And of course we can't forget Alice!

Thank you all so very much!

Patricia & Barbara

# Reflections

The opportunity to unlock your potential by reflecting on the Pieces of Advice and how to apply them begins in the following pages. They are blank right now, but as you move forward on your own journey to success write down one Piece of Advice and then identify how it can be applied in your situation and record the outcome.

This is a travel record as you move towards achieving significance in your life.

Let us know about the vistas you encounter on your journey by visiting www.1pieceofadvice.com.

*Good Luck and Bon Journée !*

# Reflections

Reflections

# Reflections